MESSAGES FROM YOUR FUTURE

The Seven Rules for
Financial, Personal and
Professional Success

LARRY FAULKNER

Published by
Faulkner Integrative Tactics (FIT)

ISBN: 978-0-692-62311-4
Library of Congress Control Number: 2016903884

Cover & Interior designed by
Rebecca Byrd Arthur, http://www.RebeccaByrd.com

Printed in the United States of America.

DEDICATION

To the public safety professionals,
the men and women who overcome adversity
each and every day in their never-ending quest
to protect their communities.

And to my wonderful wife, Lisa,
who is the secret ingredient in making
my own amazing life possible.

THE WILL TO WIN,

the desire to succeed,

the urge to reach your full potential...

these are the keys that will

unlock the door to personal excellence.

— Confucius

Introduction

THIS BOOK is very different from most financial books you will read for important reasons. It is different because our economic reality shifted after the Great Recession. Young people now start their life by going away to college filled with hope and the burning desire to make a difference in our world. Unfortunately, forces have now aligned that could very well thwart their opportunities for financial achievement. Some of these forces include the ridiculous cost of higher education, massive student loan debt, and our modern society's lack of understanding of money's role in everyone's life.

However, this book still confidently encourages the belief that with a little knowledge you have the power to create a future for yourself that you will find rewarding, fulfilling, and abounding with significant happiness. These ideal life conditions, when they come together, create what I have called an "amazing life".

An amazing life must, as a matter of necessity, contain financial abundance. This book makes the case that failing to achieve financial independence in the future is akin to giving away your freedom. Without financial independence, others will tell you what to do, how you will do it, and when you will do it—for as long as you live. This book points out that money is not everything. Nevertheless, money is necessary to creating a life that provides you with the opportunity to seek happiness and fulfillment on your own terms.

This is also a book about overcoming obstacles. For all of us, external and internal obstacles block our progress in creating the life we really desire. The external obstacles to your own amazing life may include a lack of financial knowledge, educational debt, a decrease in full-time employment opportunities, a lack of employer loyalty, the harsh reality of organizational work life, and the nonsense fed to us by the popular culture that money is the antithesis of happiness. The internal obstacles you will likely face include self-doubt, bad relationships that drag you down, and the natural tendency to simply go with the flow.

This book gives you the background you will need to begin to overcome obstacles and points out a proven path for creating the life you really desire. A life filled with accomplishment, freedom, and great relationships with your loved ones can be yours. I overcame most of these same obstacles and created my own amazing life—firmly rooted in financial independence. After applying the principles discussed in this book, my wife and I now do what we want. We travel to faraway lands, we try new things, we eat new foods, we spend time with loved ones, and we answer to no one but each other.

When I look at my friends, acquaintances, and work associates, I know that I would not trade places with any of them! Certainly I admire many of my friends and associates. I like them, I respect them, I marvel at their many accomplishments, and I even love some of them. Still, I would not trade places with a single one of them! That, my friends, is the real definition of an amazing life!

TABLE OF CONTENTS

ONE
A Message from your Future   11

TWO
Tell Me What You Want   19

THREE
Make the Goal to Win the Game   31

FOUR
Luck Meets Preparation   43

FIVE
Let Freedom Ring   57

SIX
Control Your Income   77

SEVEN
Diversity is the Spice of Life   93

EIGHT
Risking It All   117

NINE
The Battlefield of Workplace Ethics   131

TEN
Planning To Be Happy   145

ELEVEN
*Personal Experience is the Most
Expensive Investment by Far*   159

About the Author   169

ONE

A Message from your Future

Study the past, if you will divine the future.

— Confucius

Imagine that when you were older and wiser, you could send messages back in time to your younger self. These messages, e-mails from your future, let's say, would arrive suddenly in your in-box. Imagine the life-altering impact of this wisdom on your present life. These special intelligence updates—that no one else has—would bring you advance warning of all the personal misfortunes that were headed your way. Armed with that knowledge, you could easily sidestep most of life's major traps and misadventures by revising your choices, both present and long-term.

Another, even more exciting application for these messages sent from your future, is that financial, personal, and professional success could easily be yours. These emails from your future self would enable you to structure your life so that you could generate near-term and long-term prosperity. If you listen carefully to these messages, and act upon them, you can easily produce significant wealth. Thanks to this coaching from your future self, the resulting financial abundance will help you enjoy a happier and more fulfilling life.

Now, consider the monetary value of such messages. What would they be worth to you? I would have paid a fortune for them. I am absolutely certain that they would have transformed my life dramatically. Because my own misfortunes have been largely self-inflicted, the messages from my future self would have greatly enhanced my overall success. I would have structured my life to escape most of the heartache I have experienced over the years. With messages from my future guiding me, unhappy relationships, costly financial mistakes, and many other misadventures would never have materialized in the first place.

Today, you only know what you have learned from the experience and education you have received prior to this exact point in time. Your future self, however, has had many more learning opportunities. He or she has already been down the road you are just now beginning to travel. Your future self is wiser, more experienced, and much more sophisticated about all facets of life. Imagine your future self, from its well-informed perspective, transmitting its vast wisdom to enrich your present life.

Of course, we have free will and need never value e-mails from our future self. But if you knew your actions or lack of action would lead to disaster in the future, would you ignore the messages if you had them? Would you only do what feels good to you in the present?

If you continued doing nothing at all to improve your future life, even after receiving well-timed warnings, imagine how much your future self would soon begin to loathe you. In no time flat, you'd receive some additional, very nasty messages from your future self, warning you of the dire consequences headed your way.

The e-mails would explain the consequences of your laziness, your lack of attention to important issues, and your failure to consider significant facts. Would you still continue to ignore even these angry messages?

By ignoring financial messages from your future, you would also be squandering away your chance for greater wealth and personal satisfaction. Your future self has made many, many financial mistakes. Through its insight, your future self could guide you away from those same costly mistakes. Financial health is hugely important to your future, because those with minimal economic resources have very few options in life. Without options, you are not free to pursue the life you choose.

As you have probably figured out, I can't exactly get you messages from your future self—but I can bring you messages that are very close to this. Instead of contacting your future self, I have done the next best thing. I have lived a life in which I have built both personal wealth and happiness to accompany that wealth. I am now free to do as I choose, not what others might choose for me.

But the freedom to choose what you will do in life comes at a price. The price is even higher if your efforts are ineffective or misdirected—hence your need for guidance from your future, more experienced self.

I have talked with hundreds of people about their financial and personal lives. I have discussed with them how their own early actions impacted their future. I learned what made them happy, what made them unhappy, and what led to their life disasters. I also learned what led to their most wonderful successes. I have incorporated this knowledge into the things you are about to read.

Everything I have done to build wealth and happiness in my life has also been done by many others. The strategies I discuss have worked as well for others as they have for me.

In some cases, these important strategies worked even better for others, because they used them earlier in their lives and were more focused on creating the outcomes they envisioned and desired.

The strategies contained in these pages also worked for the people we read about in our history books. The same principles I will impart to you were used by some of the most famous people in history. A good example is our founding fathers. Although some of the founding fathers died paupers, others used these principles and made them work in their private and public lives—such as Benjamin Franklin and George Washington—who made their worlds better while on their own unique journeys to personal wealth.

My wife and I worked in middle class careers—I was a cop and she was a nurse. Yet, we managed to create more wealth and happiness than most people, no matter what their careers, ever manage to obtain. We basically put it all together in about 25 years—although we both started saving earlier in our lives.

Neither of us now holds a traditional wage job. She left her job as a hospital nurse at age 50. I retired from my job at 56 to work on creative projects—my own personal dream. If we created the conditions that made this possible in our lives, then you can as well. None of what I am going to show you is rocket science. What I will demonstrate to you is that working to develop a basic set of skills, combined with a moderate knowledge base supported by your own determined efforts, will unlock your almost unlimited potential in the future.

If you want to say luck plays a large part in everyone's fortune, I would certainly agree with you—up to a point. Everyone is both lucky and unlucky during their lives. You can do very little about bad luck, except minimize its damage on your life. What I hope to create, however, is the knowledge base, skill sets, and the encouragement for you to work on the preparation side of life's equation.

When proper preparation meets good luck, the joining truly captures magic in a bottle. The universe literally opens up to your wants and desires. I want you to capture financial magic, the magic of personal fulfillment, and the magic of living a satisfying life.

Your financial ability plays a central role in creating the fulfilling future you desire. Many self-help gurus and armchair philosophers tell you that money is not important; instead, you should concentrate on being happy. Quite frankly, many say this because they know almost nothing about money.

Every day, lives are damaged and incredible hardships are created by people who fail to understand how money works in their lives. People who exist with minimal financial resources may manage to be happy despite their challenges, but these people are certainly not free to do as they choose. People who understand how money works, however, are able to create significant wealth, freedom, and satisfaction in their lives.

The life conditions I have described are what I call **an amazing life.** *An amazing life* is defined as *a life filled with financial abundance, endless opportunities for happiness, and unparalleled freedom of action.* An amazing life is the central concept in the pages that follow. You can achieve an amazing life for yourself. To guide you, I have discovered a set of rules that will allow you to better direct your energy and efforts to achieve maximum results for your efforts. These rules, strategies really, will lead to a life that few others have the opportunity to experience.

My **Seven Rules for Life Success**
are simple and repeatable:

1. Try to understand what it is that you really want in life.

2. Use goal setting to obtain the life conditions you desire.

3. Create well-considered action plans to achieve your chosen goals.

4. Obtain a financial and professional (work) education.

5. Consistently upgrade both your professional and life skills.

6. Work hard to maintain your ethical and moral compass.

7. Remember that your actions today significantly impact your future.

The **Seven Rules for Life Success** are true, not because I say they are, but because it has been so throughout history. For example, Kong Qiu was born in China in 551 B.C. He was a celebrated philosopher and teacher who later became known to the western world as Confucius. One of his basic beliefs was that each of us has the ability to create the future we desire. If we obtain the necessary education, work hard, and practice self-discipline, we all have the power to succeed. His philosophy and teaching became the very foundation of Chinese thinking, philosophy, and the basis of life success for millions of people.

I tell people time and time again, your life is like a ship. As you guide your ship through dangerous channels, the shoals of disaster lie off both your port and starboard sides. You can navigate the channels of life much more easily if you will learn from those captains who sailed these waters before you. Successful people, those we read about in history books, navigated their own waters and created lives and accomplishments that still exert influence upon our world today. When these exceptional lives in history are examined from this perspective, you can easily see they honored **The Seven Rules for Life Success** on their paths to amazing lives.

TO: Present You
FROM: Future You
SUBJECT: Message from Your Future #1

Hello!

You are receiving this message from your future self, believe it or not! Time will pass. You will soon find yourself where I sit now, typing this message that will be sent back in time to you in the present.

You learned so many things on your journey from the present to the future, where I now exist. Unfortunately, so many of the things you learned during your journey were learned too late to be of maximum value to you. You certainly accomplished a lot over the years, but you could have done much better with just a little additional knowledge, experience, and focused effort. This is why I am sending you these messages.

If you choose to do so, you can build a life that is filled with financial abundance, endless opportunities for happiness, and unparalleled freedom of choice that few people are ever lucky enough to experience. You have the potential within you to become nothing less than amazing!

History has proven over and over again that The Seven Rules for Life Success work. These rules have worked for those who have achieved greatness and earned their place in our history books. The same Rules for Life Success have also worked for many average men and women whom you have never heard of. These rules or strategies created the very foundation of their amazing lives.

The messages I will be sending you are vitally important to your (our) well-being. Act upon these messages without delay.

Please help us both!

DISCOVER

Two

Tell Me What You Want

That some achieve great success, is proof to all that others can achieve it as well.

— Abraham Lincoln

I stumbled onto Rule for Life Success #1 in the middle of my junior year in high school, at around 17 years of age. Before this, I had generally been an atrocious teenager, bordering on the very brink of self-destruction. My grades were horrible (barely passing). I was experimenting with marijuana, drinking alcohol regularly, and consorting with the less-than-desirable accomplices I had chosen as friends. In short, I was headed nowhere in particular.

It began to dawn on me over several weeks that I needed to transform the way I was conducting my entire life. The only future I was preparing myself for was one of marginality. I was headed for a future of limited financial resources, filled with menial work, and few opportunities to improve my life.

I decided I wanted more. Oh sure, others had told me this same thing many times! Parents, teachers, and a few friends had expressed concern about my life choices. I ignored them, and simply did what I wanted. It felt good to shirk responsibilities and live only for moments of reckless thrill seeking.

Over the next few weeks, my unease over my life choices continued to grow. I soon resolved to change how I was living my life and what I was doing. I considered what it was that I really wanted. I decided, over a period of time, that what I really wanted was a career in law enforcement. I then contemplated how I would tackle such an ambitious goal. I developed a plan to achieve this goal. I improved my grades, got rid of my loser friends, halted my destructive behavior, and worked diligently to change the course of my life.

Once I had a clear vision of my well-designed future life, everything else began to fall easily into place. After graduating from high school, I took academic night classes, developed a reasonably good work history, and made sure I was physically fit enough to survive the rigors of the police academy. After methodically researching various police departments, I chose the one that I thought would offer me the best opportunities—professionally, personally, and financially. I was hugely successful with this goal I set for myself so many years ago.

One reason this goal worked so well for me was that it was consistent with my value system. I came from a police family, so I already shared core values that were consistent with this group. The skill sets required for the job were also consistent with my abilities. I was reasonably intelligent, very determined, and I had good interpersonal skills. The goal excited me, so I was able to maintain my enthusiasm throughout the years it took to achieve what I wanted.

D**eciding what you want (Rule for Life Success #1)** is certainly not a rule I invented. This important concept has been a basic principle for life success throughout history. Abraham Lincoln is a good example of the power that can come from defining your goals and then working diligently to achieve them. Abraham Lincoln was born on February 12, 1809 in the backwoods of Hardin County, Kentucky. His family was not political, nor famous, and they had only modest financial wealth.

In the backwoods where the Lincoln family lived, there were limited educational opportunities. Local limits on education were irrelevant for Lincoln, since his father took him out of school at a young age and kept him busy working at the family and neighboring farms. His father then pocketed all of the wages young Lincoln had earned—a practice not uncommon at that time. It is believed this experience was the beginning of Lincoln's abhorrence of slavery.

Lincoln wanted something more for his life than a simple backwoods existence filled with backbreaking labor. He wanted a life of significant financial means and a professional life that was not filled with endless physical toil.

His pioneer background gave him the mental toughness, drive, and ambition to achieve his goal. He understood that knowledge was a key to attaining the life he wanted, so at an early age he turned his efforts to the important task of securing whatever education he could. He read every book he could find or borrow as he grew up. He put considerable energy and effort into his self-education—the only option available to him during his difficult youth.

As Lincoln grew into manhood, he experienced his fair share of life's failures. He became an entrepreneur and part-owner at a local store that ran into financial trouble and soon failed. The debt he accumulated in this disastrous business venture followed Lincoln for many years, yet he continued to pursue the life that he chose and desired.

Lincoln became interested in politics as a young adult. His friends encouraged him to obtain a law degree. He embraced this goal as a means to improve his life. This new goal was well suited for his abilities and experience, given his history of self-education. It is believed that he read and studied Blackstone's Commentaries as his principle means of training for the bar exam. In 1836, at the age of 25, Lincoln took his bar examination with the Illinois Supreme Court, never having entered a school or university to study law. He passed the bar exam and received his law license. Lincoln became a corporate lawyer who made the creation of a successful law practice a priority.

Throughout his political career, Lincoln had many detractors and lost some elections. Historians agree that he made several political mistakes, but matured over the years and gained useful political skills. He developed a promising political career while maintaining a thriving law practice.

Ultimately, Abraham Lincoln was elected to the highest office in the land. His efforts in that lofty position helped to end slavery in America and save our Union. He fundamentally changed our world for the better. He accomplished every one of his goals before his tragic death.

Lincoln could have just gone with the flow and lived a perfectly ordinary life on a frontier homestead. Most people, in fact, simply go with the flow. They live the script they are handed at birth, even if they know that script will not result in the outcomes they desire. Lincoln wanted something different. He strove for and ultimately achieved, by the sheer force of his will, a radically different reality than that which he was handed at birth. His goals matched his abilities and were also consistent with his value system. He was also able to maintain a lifelong enthusiasm and passion for his goals.

Most people don't understand what it is they really want, or what it is in life that makes them happy. Consequently, many of our neighbors and friends are decidedly unhappy a good deal of the time. I can't emphasize this point enough. Look around at your family, acquaintances, and neighbors. Do they seem happy or satisfied with their lives?

Ask a few of your friends what goals they want to accomplish before they take that final dirt nap. Eight of those 10 friends won't really have an answer for you, although they may try to make one up on the spot. Ask those same 10 friends what they are passionate about in their lives. About eight out of 10 won't have a well-defined answer for you. In other words, they don't really know the destination they are seeking. When you have no particular destination in mind, you soon arrive at a destination called nowhere in particular!

Evaluating your strengths and weaknesses makes it much easier to obtain your goals. For example, if you want to be a nuclear physicist, but are mathematically challenged, this will be a difficult journey for you. Not that you can't do it; you likely could if you were determined enough. But when a goal does not match your skill sets, it will take a lot more time and work than a goal that complements the strengths and natural abilities you already possess.

To illustrate this point, a policeman I knew decided he wanted to be a doctor. He had absolutely no medical or science background. He had only a high school education and some community college classes that were unrelated to the medical field. His background did not deter him in the least. He mapped out a course of studies to correct his science and medical academic deficiencies.

Although he did well in his studies, the process took so long that he changed his mind about what he wanted. He wanted to be a doctor, he certainly had the smarts to be a doctor, but he was not willing to commit the substantial amount of time required to be a doctor.

Just for the record, his journey was not a failure! The officer's journey served to clarify his skills, abilities, and future needs. Although becoming a doctor was a praiseworthy goal, my friend discovered during his journey to achieve his goal that its future advantages to him were far outweighed by the substantial time it would take to achieve it. When embarking on this course of study, he had an intellectual understanding of the time requirements, but failed to appreciate all the ramifications of his commitment.

On further reflection, he realized that the necessary education probably would cost as much as he could earn as a physician, particularly since his income level made him ineligible for scholarships and financial aid.

Contrast this with a second officer I knew. The second officer, who was an exceptional money manager, was gifted in math, and very smart. In his late twenties, he had few college credits when he decided to pursue a business finance degree. He attended a university full-time, worked full-time, yet still managed to graduate with honors. When he received his degree, he had so many job offers that it was difficult for him to decide which one to accept. The second, more successful officer also loved the process of earning the degree, which helped him maintain his enthusiasm for his new commitment. Another major reason for his success is that his desired goal matched the skills and abilities he already possessed. At the end of his educational journey, he left the police department and became a prosperous, happy man.

Most people enjoy involving themselves in activities consistent with their talents, opposed to struggling through endeavors that are a mismatch with their natural abilities. Enjoying the process of achieving your goals is important, as the required time commitments can be quite substantial.

These two concrete examples demonstrate how it is possible for you to achieve more than 80% of the rest of the population. This can be accomplished by simply deciding what it is that you want. It is a matter of considering your natural abilities, setting a goal that excites you, and then consistently working through the steps needed to accomplish the objectives you have chosen.

Devote some time to thinking deeply about what it is that you really want in life. Where do you want to end up? What outcomes work well for you? What results would make you proud of the life you have lived? This requires concentration and organized thought. Casual and fleeting attention to this objective simply won't do the job.

Many people only decide overall career objectives. This is falling well short of the mark for creating your own amazing life. It is preferable to consider your financial goals, personal goals, and relationship goals as pieces of the puzzle. All of these pieces fit together to compose your life. These three categories blend together to create the satisfaction or dissatisfaction you will feel each day. If one aspect of your life falls out of balance, it has the potential to crash the other critical components that compose your life. For instance, a poor relationship with your significant other will have a negative impact upon your job performance. A poor work situation will also impact your personal relationships.

If you don't believe you can set goals for your personal relationships, you are wrong. Twenty-five years ago, I was sitting in my dining room. I had just suffered two failed marriages, one right after the other. Neither of them lasted longer than a few years. I was convinced that neither divorce was my fault (strangely enough, both women now live perfectly happy lives without me in them). I was at peace with both divorce decisions; however, I had just spent considerable time, energy, and money on these two failed relationships.

This was completely unacceptable, not to mention massively expensive. There had to be a better way than my current decision-making paradigm!

My perspective made a 180 degree turn on that fateful day at my dining room table. I finally realized that I had to accept responsibility for selecting a compatible person to be my significant other. This was my issue and no one else's responsibility or problem.

I had been selecting women whose value systems were at odds with my own. I discovered, after considerable analysis, that my value system was hugely important to me. The women I was choosing had values that were decidedly different from my own, probably because their backgrounds were so vastly dissimilar to mine. My selection process had to change if I was going to create the future I wanted.

I had been leaving the entire process of love and romance to chance. I realized that my set of potential candidates included only those I happened to meet by chance (long before the process of internet dating/matching sites). When I reached this conclusion, I immediately wrote a list of the qualities I wanted in a significant other.

Once that list was completed, I knew the truth about the person I really wanted. No longer would I be leaving this process to chance, as I now had a detailed profile of the woman I was seeking.

I am not suggesting you conjure up creepy, unsavory notions or behaviors in connection with this task. I am simply suggesting that you develop a deeper understanding of what it is that you are looking for (or actually need) in a significant other. After I completed this enlightening exercise, I then began searching for a more suitable companion who met my criteria in places where she was likely to be found.

I was looking for a smart, independent woman who would be loving and supportive, but did not need me to make her life complete. In other words, I was looking for someone who was already succeeding in her own life, as opposed to a rescue project. I wanted an exciting, dynamic partner that would keep me engaged.

I avoided cultivating serious relationships with women whose personalities and circumstances were at odds with my established criterion. I did find a woman who closely matched the attributes from my list and can now confirm that these were the exact qualities I wanted and needed in a significant other.

The list I created had power, as it defined and clarified for me what I wanted. My meticulous attention to this process enabled me to recognize these desirable traits when I saw them. I had the courage to pursue my wife once I met her, because I understood how important she could be in my life. Creating a fulfilling relationship with a significant other makes a tremendous difference as you create your own amazing future.

Once we were together, we set goals, envisioning what we wanted for our vibrant future relationship. By doing my part (the only part I can do) to create a great relationship, she was encouraged to do her part to make the relationship work. If I had simply left this part to chance (doing only whatever I wanted), who knows what our relationship might be now? Instead, we have a satisfying relationship of give and take in an environment of mutual respect—exactly what I wanted!

The very act of writing down what you want to achieve ignites a powerful force in your life. Whether that power comes from within, or from the larger universe, I do not really know.

I can only say this process has worked for me and others time and time again.

I approach this endeavor by making a list of my goals and sub-goals. I then list the steps involved in achieving my chosen goals. Somehow, this process taps into the power of the universe and things begin to happen. My goals begin to move forward.

You also have the power to choose your financial future. All you need is the determination to decide what financial resources you want in your future and the courage to do what it takes to seize them. I use the term courage, because it will (never doubt it) require significant work and effort on your part. Some of your success, as in all things, is impacted by chance occurrences. Some people get dealt a crappy hand in life—like an illness that saps all your financial resources. There is nothing we can do about bad luck except work to minimize its influence on our lives. Bad luck, however, is generally not the norm.

The vast majority of people have the opportunity to decide what they want their future to become. I use the term opportunity, because many simply do not bother to decide what they want. This is because deciding the direction of your future requires planning, commitment, and painstaking effort.

These three things (planning, commitment, and effort) separate those who succeed financially, and in all other aspects of their lives, from those who surrender to living with mediocre results. Deciding what it is that makes you happy, what your goals will be, and taking positive actions to achieve your chosen outcomes are the foundation of building your own amazing life.

TO: Present You
FROM: Future You
SUBJECT: Message from Your Future #2

Hello:

You have the power to actually choose success and prosperity. You can decide to work in a great career, enjoy terrific personal relationships, and take pleasure in creating financial wealth in your future. All of these goals are within your reach. The most important step in obtaining the future you want is deciding what it is that you really desire. What do you value? What kind of person do you want to be in your future?

Deciding what you want in life is much easier if what you desire matches your natural talents and abilities. Consider how this list applies to the outcomes you choose:

- Is the goal consistent with your value system?
- Is the goal consistent with your natural abilities?
- Can you maintain enthusiasm for the goal over a long period of time?

Devote some time to deciding where it is you want to go, what you want to accomplish, and what you want to create in your life. Write out a list of your goals. This will take a few weeks, but that's okay. This exercise does not tie you to these original goals forever. Some goals will be cast aside, some goals will change, and some goals will become even more important as time moves forward.

Once you have decided where you are headed, your path will become clearer to you. Once your destination is understood, concentrate on planning your path to achieving your goals, commit yourself to obtaining them, and maintain your effort consistently to achieve success.

Deciding and understanding what it is that you want are the first steps in building the foundation for an exceptional future. Make well-considered choices, ones that are consistent with your abilities and talents. Once these choices are made, you are well on the road to realizing a life that is nothing less than amazing.

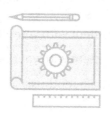

CONSTRUCT

THREE

Make the Goal to Win the Game

Obstacles are those frightful things you see when you take your eyes off the goal.

— Henry Ford

I worked on a variety of assignments during my 32 years as a police officer. I had enjoyed the job, but it was time to begin moving up through my department's chain of command. Promotions in the civil services system involve competitive testing based on material that is relevant to the higher rank.

Candidates receive a list of literature on police subjects, study the literature, and then take a comprehensive test covering that material. The best score wins the first job opening and so on through the list. Doing poorly means you get nothing for your effort. You can literally study for weeks and weeks, take the test, and never be promoted.

The first time I took a promotional test, my attempt coincided with the City's introduction of an assessment center into the promotional testing process. An assessment center rates candidates after observing them performing various skills, tasks, and exercises. These assessment centers are typically combined with the traditional, knowledge-based written test, to establish a candidate eligibility list for promotion.

I earned one of the top scores on the traditional written exam, but then performed terribly (in my opinion) on the new assessment center tasks. I was finally promoted, but ranked well down on the promotional list.

This was a new process in Dayton, Ohio. My experience with the assessment center was not unique. Lots of my peers had similar experiences and were preforming poorly in this new promotional process.

What separated my future success from other officers' who never rose through the ranks is that I was determined to learn how to maximize my performance in this testing arena and read everything I could find in books and articles covering assessment centers. I also located and talked to assessment center raters (observers who numerically score candidates based on their performance) to learn more about the process and what the raters were looking for in a candidate.

I learned specific assessment center performance skills. I pestered friends and relatives to act as practice assessors and ask me questions about how I would handle various scenarios typically covered in assessment center testing. I practiced answering those questions in a coherent and engaging manner.

During the next promotional test, I promptly crushed the assessment center tasks, as well as the written exam. I catapulted toward the top of the promotion list and received the next promotion in short order. This promotion improved my life, as I had hoped it would. It gave me more control over my work environment, provided me with additional income, and created even greater opportunities in my future. In fact, my life improved after each promotion within the department.

Rule for Life Success # 2 explains that *we can use goal setting and achievement to obtain the life conditions we desire.* This concept, as history will show, is certainly nothing new. For example, on July 30, 1863, Henry Ford was born on his family's farm in Dearborn, Michigan. Like Abraham Lincoln, he was deeply unsatisfied with farm life and the backbreaking work it required. Ford wanted something different and more fulfilling for his life.

Young Ford had an extremely high mechanical aptitude. He took apart his toys, watches, or anything else he could find. Surprisingly, however, unlike most children, he could also put all of them back together again.

Ford developed a particular fascination with the steam engine, which was at the height of engine technology at that particular time. From these early experiences, Ford developed a driving ambition to work with machines. He ultimately used his mechanical talents to escape farm life for good by taking a job in Detroit, Michigan.

Once in Detroit, Ford was irresistibly drawn to the newly developed ethanol-powered engine. The idea of an engine powering a horseless carriage fascinated him. Thus, he decided upon a goal to start and run an automobile manufacturing company.

He used his natural drive and ambition to start his earliest manufacturing companies that produced horseless carriages. Each of these companies failed financially. Each horseless carriage had to be made by hand, a very expensive process that severely limited his market. Ford refused to give up and retained significant excitement for his goal. He worked in a variety of places, learning more and more with each new job.

Ford soon leveraged his automobile racing success into another business venture. He used his racing wins to attract investors to his new Ford Motor Company. Once established, Ford changed his world by perfecting the assembly line and many other manufacturing processes. He also redesigned the gasoline engine to make it more suitable for large-scale production. His efforts, coincidentally, also significantly improved the gas engine's performance.

Ford's innovations revolutionized our world by creating processes that made the automobile affordable to the masses. Once affordable, automobiles became widely popular. Ford soon became one of the wealthiest men in history. He achieved every goal he had set back in his youth.

Established principles separate goals from mere daydreaming or wishful thinking. Goals, as opposed to passing desires or daydreams, have a specific structure. They must have specific benchmarks to measure achievement.

Once a benchmark is set, you must set your timetable for achieving your goal. When will you be able to achieve it? You should be able to determine a realistic timetable with a little thought. Write the deadline next to your goal. Then, write the same completion date at the bottom of your paper.

Next, write down the detailed action steps (sub goals) that you believe will lead you to the final outcome you desire. List as many action steps as you can. This task typically requires a little research to determine the best action steps to achieve your goal.

Write down each of these action steps under your final goal. Add projected completion dates to all of your action steps. What you have now developed is a step-by-step plan with an anticipated completion date for your goal. Then you need only work through these action steps to create the success you are seeking.

My **Seven Rules for Life Success, Rule #3,** states *you should create a well-considered action plan to achieve your chosen goals.* The steps listed above will give you a workable action plan—in its simplest form. Your plan to achieve your goal is, of course, subject to modifications as conditions develop and change. Consider the elevated strategic advantage your action steps will give you over someone who has not developed a defined plan. Capture this advantage by designing your own action plan.

Some people may think this is very simplistic stuff. "Everyone with any common sense knows about goal setting." I strongly disagree! If that statement were true, why are so many people frustrated by their jobs, home lives, and various other troublesome conditions. They hate their jobs, they hate their spouses, and they sometimes hate their entire lives. They are grumpy, moody, and generally exude a bad attitude toward anyone who is unlucky enough to encounter them.

Typically, the main reason so many people continue to endure this unhappy existence is that changing their lives requires a lot of effort, planning, and concentrated thought. The actions necessary to accomplish a goal typically move them away from their comfort zone and normal routine. When they are reluctant to exert the effort to change, these unhappy individuals remain stuck in their joyless cycle.

If you think this is a good plan, but are hesitant to actually write out your goals, sub goals, and the accompanying timetables, remember **Rule for Life Success #3**. *Don't fail to take this extra step. Write out your goals. When you write down your goals, you can hold in your hand a tangible document that embodies the ideas that are propelling you into the future you imagined. The list is the physical evidence of an already changing reality. This document also serves as a flexible reference tool and a visible reminder of your commitment to your goal.*

No matter what you do in life, only two options exist to change what you perceive to be a bad situation. Both options are reasonably good ones. The first option is to change your attitude. This is difficult, but doable—unless changing your

attitude conflicts with your core values. If it does, then changing your attitude simply won't work for you. You will only be
suppressing issues that will soon bubble back to the surface.

The second option is to change your life by improving the
conditions that have become untenable. This is done through
goal setting and working through an action plan to achieve the
change you desire.

If you don't like your life, simply change it! Goal setting
and goal achievement is the vehicle by which this work gets
done—there is no other way. My very smart wife has a saying,
"Plan ahead to get ahead!"

If you are not planning, scripting, researching, and working
through your plans, then you are letting life's currents carry you
downstream. Sometimes this works out, yet most of the time it
leads to very substandard results. If you have invested the time
to read this material, you should naturally want more, demand
more, and expect more. That means that you must also plan
more and work more to achieve your own exceptional life!

Several years ago I had a regularly scheduled lunch with
a police lieutenant. As long-time friends, we had traveled
through the various police ranks, more or less, together. These
regular get-togethers provided us with a refreshing diver-
sion from our stress-filled days. He had worked very hard to
achieve his promotion to lieutenant after waiting several years
for this position to open.

During our lunch the lieutenant said, "When I was promoted
to lieutenant, I thought the promotion would make me happy.
After being a lieutenant now for a while, I wonder if this is really
all there is to it?" He meant, of course, that he wasn't much happier now than he had been before he received the promotion.

I asked him if he liked being a sergeant more than being a
lieutenant—begging the solution to simply return to his previ-

ous rank of sergeant. He admitted that he liked the lieutenant position better than his old sergeant position. It provided him more decision-making authority and control over his life.

Yet he had expected that achieving this goal (promotion to lieutenant) would make him happy. After achieving this goal, he wasn't much happier than he was before.

This lieutenant, like a lot of other people, was under the mistaken impression that achieving a goal (getting promoted to the rank of lieutenant in this instance) would create significant happiness in his life. He was dismayed to discover it didn't.

Achieving a goal is not the same thing as achieving happiness. We work to achieve our goals to furnish us with the ability to generate conditions that will result in a more gratifying and fulfilling life—big picture stuff. Achieving goals creates an opportunity for our happiness to flourish and grow in the present and the future. That is not the same as achieving happiness. So when you achieve your goals, don't expect some massive wave of happiness to overtake you—it simply won't.

Happiness is something that occurs only in the present. You can be happy no matter what happens—or at least there are some people who can. Being happy is largely our own personal responsibility. This can be a hard concept to accept. Setting and achieving financial goals is worth doing to make our future life easier and more fulfilling in the long run.

Achieving financial goals grants you the freedom to choose your future rather than having circumstances dictate it for you. Meeting or exceeding your financial goals, will not, in and of itself make you happy. Financial abundance, however, can significantly contribute to your prospects for happiness.

The future you seek lies across a deep chasm. Close in actual distance, but sometimes very hard to reach. The goal is to build a bridge across this chasm to seize the future you desire. Bridge building is not always an easy business. It takes courage and perseverance. You can get battered and bruised as you construct your bridge across this chasm of time. Many people don't have the stomach for the job or the emotional maturity to be successful at it. But I believe in you! I believe you can achieve success if you will only believe that you can!

The brick and mortar for your bridge across this chasm is made up of your commitment to your goals, personal responsibility for the outcomes of your life, a large dose of enthusiasm, and a decent work ethic. Positive action steps that honor your talents and a large dose of perseverance will separate the winners from the losers in the future. The fact that you are reading this book and considering these concepts means that you have already started building your bridge.

It happens quite a bit, through no fault of your own, that a goal you were committed to suddenly leaves you feeling cold and disinterested. Although goal achievement cannot make you happy, working hard to achieve a goal when you have lost the enthusiasm for it, will definitely make you decidedly unhappy. As a matter of fact, left unchecked, this unhappy situation has the potential to overshadow your life.

Decide what it is that you need to make yourself happier. If your goal has become less appealing, no longer excites you, or generally fades in relevance to your life, simply abandon that goal. You can alter your plans with little penalty as the situation on the ground unfolds. This is a lesson every good general knows when he or she rides into battle.

Things suddenly and unexpectedly change. You change! Plans go awry and goals become impossible, or are no longer worth the effort required to follow through with them. Set new goals that match who you have become over time.

Changing your goals is not failure, but the evolution of self. Honor yourself and your journey by abandoning good goals that inexplicably go bad. There is no need to feel regretful about this. Move on to other goals that rekindle your enthusiasm and interest.

This information about abandoning a goal gone bad is not a permission slip to abandon every goal you set due to laziness. That is certainly not what I am saying. What I am saying is that your life changes you as you live it. Working action steps to achieve your goals changes you. You will not be the same person you are now in ten, twenty, or thirty years. Goals must keep pace with who you are.

Goal achievement should always be celebrated. Even every sub goal achievement should be celebrated. You have successfully battled the forces aligned against you in the universe and bent those forces to your will. Your own particular desires and personal vision of your future is coming to life. Such victories should never be taken lightly. They are, after all, milestones on your path to an amazing future.

TO: Present You

FROM: Future You

SUBJECT: Message from Your Future #3

Hello:

I have new information that will not only improve your present life, but also the life you will soon live in your future. Goal setting and goal attainment are essential skills for developing an amazing life. I encourage you to use goal setting to create a better version of yourself.

Goals have a generally accepted structure:

- Goals are written.

- Goals must have specific achievement benchmarks.

- Goals must have realistic timetables.

One of the most important messages I am sending you from the future is that you should take charge of your life and accept total responsibility for it. Ultimately, you control the majority of the outcomes you experience—both now and in your future. Try to look ahead and decide what outcomes you actually desire rather than waiting for the tide to rush you into the land of marginality.

Planning, goal setting, and working through actions steps will allow you the freedom to live the life that you choose.

You must commit yourself entirely to seizing your freedom—particularly your financial freedom. Plan ahead to get ahead!

Remember to celebrate every success along your personal road to the future you desire. Want more, plan more, achieve more, love more, and ultimately you will be more! This is the path to an amazing life!

VISION

FOUR

Luck Meets Preparation

Before anything else, preparation is the key to success.

— Alexander Graham Bell

Ten years after joining the police department, my attitude was bad. In fact, it was very bad. My job irritated me. The organizational bureaucracy of the police department was nearly overwhelming. I had been promoted to sergeant, but even this job now seemed old and stale! The Ohio Police and Fire Retirement System had implemented a change that kept personnel in their jobs for a much longer period. This change caused all upward movement in my police department to come to a screeching halt.

After an extended period of brooding, I analyzed my state of mind. Why was I feeling this way? (Rule #1 for Life Success—what do I really want?). Finally, after several weeks of self-reflection, I came to the heart of the problem. The real underlying issue was that I was feeling trapped, not by the bottleneck in promotions that held me in place, but by my lack of formal education and job training.

I had slightly less than a two-year education at a community college instead of a four-year college degree. The education I had was adequate for my current job, but my inadequate education severely limited my future opportunities.

Being big on planning (**Rule #2 for Life Success**), I began to devise a plan to overcome my educational deficits. I listed on paper where I found myself in the present. I then imagined the future I wanted to create for myself. I created action steps to obtain the outcomes I desired—**Rule for Life Success #3**. My wife and I discussed, and then slightly modified, my plan. I committed myself to **Rule #4 for Life Success** which states, "*Obtain a financial and professional (work) education.*"

I taped my action plan to my bathroom mirror. I reviewed those steps every morning when I got out of bed. I then forged ahead with my plan to change my own reality. The plan involved securing both a higher education and increasing my technical work skills through training.

Whether I was going to use the formal education and improved work skill sets to advance in my current job, or in another police department, was yet to be determined. Either way, this plan would provide me with the options I desired.

To achieve my goals, I began taking one or two classes at a time from a local accredited university. I generally could not take more than one class at a time because of their significant draw upon my time—my wife and I were also raising three boys. Several years later, the entire family attended my college graduation.

I suddenly realized that I had been so busy working through my plan that I no longer gave much thought to the work irritations that had so bothered me previously. When I was occupied with my plan, the job was not the grind it had once been. My mind simply did not have the energy or time to waste thinking about such things. Essentially, I changed my entire world by changing myself.

When I completed my academic goals, my employer had finally cycled back around to promoting new command personnel. Interestingly enough, the police department had also begun to institute new educational requirements for higher ranks.

These prerequisites were unknown to our department when I began focusing on my academic goals. These new requirements limited the promotional pool, making my success even easier. Each new rank also came with a significant pay raise that my wife and I immediately rolled into our savings and investment plan.

Please notice that I could have decided that what I wanted was the police department to change its bureaucratic ways so that I might be happier. That is, of course, the wrong answer! When you set goals and change your life conditions, you are really changing yourself and your ability to enhance your life. Only after you change yourself can you expect to alter your outside world.

In my case, the real problem was my lack of formal education and training. If you have analyzed your problem and come up with an answer that doesn't start with changing yourself, you have most likely missed the mark.

As an example, if I hated my relationship with my spouse, what could I do to change this reality? I can't change my spouse—ever! Instead, I can only have the power to change myself:

- Change my attitude
- Change responses
- Change my habits
- Change my marital status

When I change the first few things on this list, it typically will create the conditions to encourage my spouse to change her responses to me. Or, if I move forward with a divorce, it will eventually change both our realities. The answer must always begin with changing yourself.

Luck meets preparation and creates magic! Or, as my lovely wife says, *"Plan ahead to get ahead!"* Our friends hear this phrase from us repeatedly. *Prepare yourself with the proper education, training, and relevant work experience and luck tends to follow.* It happens time and time again.

My graduate degree in evidence-based policing is another example of luck meets preparation. Coincidentally, this just happened to be the skill most valued by our new police chief. The preparations I made propelled me forward within the police organization.

To build the amazing life you want in your future (the very purpose for reading this book) you must continually work to improve your annual income. To improve your income, you must obtain better jobs to gain the additional funds that the better positions bring.

I am not suggesting that you run yourself into the ground and have a heart attack on an endless treadmill of achievement. There is balance in all things (See Chapter 10 on happiness). I'm merely pointing out that the goal is to eventually leave working for others, on their terms, behind you. Your ultimate goal is independence from the wage-based employment rat race.

The Rules for Life Success in this book have applied universally across history. **Rule #4 for Life Success, *obtaining a financial and professional education,*** is just as important today as it has been throughout history. Alexander Graham Bell, for example, was born March 3, 1847, in Edinburgh, Scotland. He certainly did not start his career with the invention of the telephone. Instead, he began by working and researching in the field of reproducing human speech, using both mechanical and electromagnetic technology to assist the deaf.

For years he studied and assisted others, working at the cutting edge of research in human speech reproduction. Only after working in this field for years did he advance beyond the known frontier of technical knowledge. Bell's patent for an electromagnetic device that transmitted human speech was granted on March 7, 1876. His prior research and knowledge had resulted in the creation of the telephone. This was the most valuable patent ever filed by the patent office during that time period.

While Bell invented the new electromagnetic speech reproduction processes that created the telephone, America had entered its Age of Invention. Pioneers such as Thomas Edison, Henry Ford, and George Washington Carver changed our world through their unique innovations.

Bell's preparation in the field of speech reproduction, combined with the new technology of this age, merged to create a revolutionary advancement in science. In short, Bell's preparation transported him beyond the brink of known knowledge, thereby cementing his place in history.

In light of Bell's immensely valuable patent, hordes of envious people who claimed that Bell had stolen their scientific works for his invention attacked him. In all, over 600 lawsuits were filed against him. Several of them went to the Supreme Court of the United States. Bell won all the challenges! Bell won them primarily because he could readily document his very extensive research in this field over the years. He had done all the background work to make his invention possible. Further, his challengers had filed their lawsuits 18 months or more after his invention had become a working reality.

Bell's challengers lacked Bell's history of research and preparation in this realm of science. The court was very impressed by Bell's longstanding work in this field. Obviously, in so many ways, Bell's preparation created the wonderful success he later enjoyed.

Alexander Graham Bell honored the Rules for Life Success:

#4. Obtained a financial and professional (work related) education

#5. Consistently upgraded both his work and life coping skills

Honoring these rules is critically important, because our work world continuously evolves and changes. In America, for example, workers are becoming more and more like the ronin of medieval Japan. Ronin roamed the countryside of feudal Japan because their masters had either died or cast them out.

Once the ronin were without a master to employ them, they had to earn a living on their own. They roamed the countryside and took whatever work they could get—typically using their sword skills. Today's American ronin (workers) roam from job to job across America in search of masters willing to take them in.

During the Great Recession, employers came to believe (rightly or wrongly) that the path to corporate profitability was to reduce the number of employees in order to increase their company's profit margins. The companies also began to cut health care benefits to improve their bottom line. They began to discard pension plan obligations to reduce their debt in the future. These cost-reducing trends, designed to boost corporate profitability, continue today.

The only practical strategy to be successful in our current economy is to consistently work each day to increase your work and life coping skills. Every day, you must strive to be a better version of yourself.

Most people, of course, won't do this. Consistently working to upgrade your work-related skills can be hard work, requiring a great deal of thought. People tend to be creatures of habit and resist breaking their normal routines. The human tendency to stay stuck in a routine will hinder your success and diminish your value to your employer. If you allow **Rules for Life Success #4 and #5** to guide you, you will be the dynamic employee who is always more informed, more skilled, and upwardly mobile.

Several long-time friends and I had lunch recently. This allowed our little group to reconnect and catch up on each other's lives. One of the men at the table, a local business owner, told our group that he wanted to expand his business. To have time to expand, he needed a new employee to free him from some routine work in his business office. He had been unable to find the right person.

What he needed was a part-time employee who was technically savvy enough to answer e-mails and work on social media marketing. The person who received the job could easily do much (but not all) of the work from their home.

The business owner found that the younger people he recruited were technically savvy enough to do the job, but had trouble meeting deadlines and other routine work responsibilities. The older people he had hired were very dependable, but had virtually no technical skills. Unfortunately, he has remained unable to find someone to fill this important position.

Obviously, both groups needed to upgrade their work skills. Neither group seemed to be honoring **Rules for Life Success #4 and #5.** The younger people needed to learn work dependability skills—yes, this is a learned skill. The older workers need to become current with computer and social media skills. This example illustrates just how easy it is to use career preparation skills to stand out from the crowd and succeed where others flounder.

After obtaining the correct technical qualifications to land a job, communication skills are the next most important ability that any worker could possess—no matter the industry. Working for an employer is a team sport—period! Virtually every job involves extensive teamwork.

Some people who, essentially, work alone, or those with outstanding technical skills may believe that developing good communication skills is a waste of time. That is simply not true. Even if you only interact with a supervisor on occasion, you are still participating in a team sport. Even people who are self-employed require good communication skills to work with the customers who utilize their businesses.

Communication skills are required to:

- Communicate effectively using both verbal and non-verbal techniques.

- Engage in effective teamwork to accomplish your company's goals.

- Support and motivate fellow team members.

- Accomplish your assigned tasks and goals.

- Demonstrate leadership in the workplace.

- Build personal and professional networks.

- Create work alliances that are required to accomplish your work unit's assigned goals.

Creating alliances in the workplace (part of communication) does not equate with petty office politics and is not merely a waste of time. Alliances in the workplace enable you to get your work accomplished. Interactions with your network of alliances create relationship bonds with other company members who will support your efforts.

The bonds you forge may also provide you with future opportunities you hadn't imagined—such as a promotion or a better assignment within your current organization. When team members leave to accept more desirable employment opportunities, they may pave the way for you to join them at their new organization. The opportunities and connections you can create by building alliances are absolutely essential. Building alliances always begins with good communication skills.

I can easily prove the importance of good people skills with this phrase, "Bad bosses are common and good bosses are rare." The fact that so many people identify with this statement demonstrates that people skills are not nearly as common as we might believe. It also explains why people skills are always in high demand at the workplace.

A bad boss may communicate with you in a negative tone, fail to engage you, and fail to inspire you to achieve the work unit's goals. Bad bosses are not good communicators! In fact, they barely qualify as human beings.

How many examples of bad bosses do you recognize in the list below?

- A boss that is exceptionally self-absorbed.

- A boss who favors political expediency over any real progress in the organization.

- A boss who is absolutely devoid of any creativity and also forbids you to unleash your own creativity.

- A boss who lacks commitment to the job, which leads to a natural lack of commitment to support his team.

- A boss who makes no effort to recall the problems faced by subordinates, nor to realize how difficult their jobs can be at times.

- A boss with a total commitment to tradition, even when tradition is obviously failing to solve new challenges faced by your work unit
- A boss who enjoys bulling subordinates and peers.
- A boss that is simply (by your own evaluation) crazy as a mad-hatter.
- A boss that creates havoc through passive-aggressive behavior that pits peers against each other.

Communication skills are arguably even more important in your personal life. Communication lies at the very root of personal/family relationships. We all have people in our lives that are very poor communicators. The truth is, these people suffer the consequences of this deficit every day. Divorces, estranged family members, and hardships rooted in marital discord are problems that can typically be traced back to poor communication skills. The good news is that there are many books, classes, trainers, and articles on improving communications.

An important component of communication is the ability to write well. The written word is still king in the workplace. Your writing ability, in the form of a resume, is the first thing a potential employer evaluates. Also, in the work world, if it isn't written, it didn't happen. If you feel your writing skills need upgrading, this is an easy fix. Plenty of seminars, books, and formal educational opportunities abound that specialize in business writing.

Leadership is another essential skill in the workplace. Leadership is required at every level. Leaders are good at communicating and problem solving, and they don't whine. A leader goes above and beyond, and is genuinely committed to outcomes that serve both the company and its employees. Leaders are also just and moral—so people don't mind following their lead (see Chapter 9).

Workers who find themselves stuck with a bad boss or a terrible job feel trapped (this is one of the most important concepts you will read in this book). Workers feel trapped because they are not prepared to leave their employer. Typically, trapped workers are held in place financially (can't do without income even for a short period of time) or can't find a similar job elsewhere (skill deficit).

Keeping your skills updated, obtaining the proper academic education, and keeping your personal finances in order (meaning low debt) will provide you with more options in the rough and tumble work world. More options will allow you to jump work units or even jump to a different employer. Failing to take charge of your future, however, condemns you to a lifetime of working for bad bosses or in jobs you could very well hate.

Educational opportunities are offered in all of the skills covered in this chapter. Workers without the skills listed in these pages face a limited future. Unlock your potential, become a student of workplace skills, and create your own amazing life.

TO: Present You
FROM: Future You
SUBJECT: Message from Your Future #4

Hello:

I am asking you to walk a path of continual improvement. The way you prepare yourself to succeed in your future is by obtaining the necessary career-based education. In the work world, employees have become similar to the Japanese ronin of medieval times who wandered Japan looking for a master.

Workers seem to hold a job only temporarily. This means you must always be preparing for your next job. It is up to you to keep your job skills, abilities, and education on the cutting edge so that you can leave your employer (if necessary) and seek better employment elsewhere. Every day you must work, dress, train, and act like you are competing for your next job.

Technical work skills are always in demand and are every bit as important as formal academics—you must possess both. After the required technical skills, the most important workplace skill is communication. Working at a job is a team sport and you are judged from that perspective by your peers and bosses.

Create friends and allies, not enemies and detractors, within your workplace. The primary vehicle for creating allies in your workplace is through the expert use of interpersonal communication skills—both verbal and nonverbal. Creating allies may pave the path for a better work environment and future career opportunities.

Other important technical skills include business writing and leadership. Without this set of work-centered skills, your future is severely limited. Classes, books, and seminars are offered almost everywhere on these important topics. Become a student of these disciplines.

Communication is just as important in your personal life. If you get lazy with communication skills, both your loved ones and you will suffer the consequences. Failed relationships are created every day due to a lack of effective communication. Failed relationships also can create massive financial hardships. Become a serious student of interpersonal communication and take the time to learn its finer points.

Failing to obtain superior work skills can trap you in less-than-ideal jobs or positions. A strategy of continual improvement enables you to obtain increasingly better jobs. Obtaining a better job could easily lead to an increase in your annual income. You should, therefore, strive to be a better version of yourself each day. Continual improvement is the path to amazing!

KNOWLEDGE

FIVE

Let Freedom Ring

Those who would give up essential liberty to purchase a little temporary safety deserve neither liberty nor safety.

— Benjamin Franklin

The promotion of a police officer to the rank of sergeant brings with it a substantial pay raise, along with many additional responsibilities. Each newly promoted group of sergeants is typically kept together for a few weeks of training before they start their new work assignments. As a division commander, with a long and successful career behind me, I always made it a point to drop by one of these training sessions to talk with each group of new sergeants.

The young faces of the men and women at the large table looked up at me as I walked into the training room at the police academy. I smiled and greeted them as I took a standing position at the front of the room. After congratulating them once again on obtaining their promotions, I talked about the importance of their new responsibilities.

I urged them to quickly learn the skills necessary to fulfill their new roles. At the conclusion of my brief talk, I also encouraged each new supervisor to save the raise that he or she would receive from this promotion and put that raise into an appropriate retirement account for the future.

Surprisingly (at least surprisingly to me because of the formal setting), one of the newly promoted sergeants immediately spoke up. "That's not going to happen," he retorted. "After all, you don't go into this career to get rich!" I smiled, thanked them all for giving me their attention, and politely left the training room to go about my day. After all, I had learned from my previous experience that hardheaded people must learn things the hard way!

The outspoken sergeant's declaration of belief was, of course, entirely ridiculous. If the principle he boldly put forth during that training session were true—that only dedication to the career and the job of policing are important—the chief of police would be a happy man indeed. He should, if this notion were actually true, immediately announce, "I'm going to cut your pay in half and return this money to the citizens of our city who worked so hard for it." Can you imagine the immediate outcry a 50% cut in pay would elicit from his officers? The chief could then say, "No worries, as you really didn't come into this career field to get rich anyway!" Why stop at a 50% pay cut? Why not decree that the police department would now pay their officers only $1.00 a year for their work? After all, if you chose a police career, the money is not an important factor to you. The sergeant's premise was absolute silliness!

I am quite sure the response I received from the sergeant had nothing at all to do with the recommendation I made. It's my best bet that the young man, along with many others who voice his sentiments, have leveraged themselves and their families' futures to the maximum. Too bad for their poor families!

The new sergeant probably needed this pay raise just to cover his monthly bills. His comments were undoubtedly an attempt to make himself feel better regarding his inability to control his money and to secure his family's financial future.

He also probably felt his comments and philosophy absolved him of the responsibility to make his and his family's life financially sound—in the present or in the future. This way, he can believe his lack of financial success is not his fault, because he is altruistically dedicated to his job. This philosophy is, of course, simply rubbish!

There is only one reason to have a job. The reason to work at a job is to make an income. Period! If you don't need the income, or think income is not important, you can skip the entire job process and get on with doing things that fulfill you personally—like volunteering in your community. Most people do need a job, however, to fund their lives and the lives of their loved ones.

With a job, there are three considerations. The first consideration is making enough money to fund your life in a manner that is reasonable to you. If you don't make enough money, you will not be committed to the job and will leave when a better opportunity presents itself—no matter how altruistic you are. Just ask employees who only make minimum wage if they are willing to leave their jobs for better paying positions. Careful, as the employees may trample you as they run out the door to seize them.

The second consideration for a job is being able to stand the work and the working conditions that come along with it. Some jobs are so toxic and horrible that the job is not worth any possible wage—particularly since you could probably find a similar paying job elsewhere that is less toxic or damaging. Even if a job is toxic, most people must still find another job before they can quit the one they have, because they require a constant flow of money to fund their lives.

Finally, only after the first two factors are considered and dealt with does a person's dedication to the mission of a profession (such as helping others) become a consideration. Don't get me wrong, when you sincerely believe in the mission of your employer, it is a wonderful thing—as long as you are paid enough to support what you consider a reasonable lifestyle.

Understanding that a job is actually about the money is something you learn over time. It is part of your overall financial education. **Rule for Life Success #4** stresses *the importance of obtaining a financial education.* Like Abraham Lincoln's education, a financial education is something that you must essentially obtain on your own. Unfortunately, in America today, the average citizen now knows so little about money and finances that few people are available to teach you about controlling the money in your life.

The lack of a financial education severely handicaps and cripples so many people—perhaps most people. Without a financial education, you are likely headed for life filled with endless work that offers very limited freedom.

Rule for Life Success #7 states that *your actions today significantly impact your future.* This young sergeant failed to understand, or didn't wish to understand, that I was living proof of the principles I had just presented to his group. When I retired, just a few months later, it was not to take another job to continue servicing my personal debt balances. It was, instead, to live the life that I had chosen.

It is an often-quoted phrase that money is the root of all evil. Money is not evil in and of itself. It is simply a tool like an axe, chainsaw, knife, or firearm. Money is designed to perform a function. It is what is done with money, or to obtain money, that can create problems. I don't love money, nor, covet it at all costs.

What I do love, however, is freedom. Money has the ability to provide me with the precious freedom to do as I wish (within the bounds of reason and financial common sense). Most people can't do what they want. They must work until they are unable to physically work another day.

If you think these older workers like the situation they find themselves in, just ask one of them! The older workers that I have spoken with wish they did not have to work at their ages. They would certainly retire if they were financially able to do so.

My wife and I built unparalleled freedom in a future that we custom designed for ourselves. When we retired, we promptly went to San Francisco and visited one of our sons living in that area. My wife and I then went to Alaska on an extended adventure. We then traveled to Las Vegas, lived in Virginia for a short time to visit family, and we recently returned from an extended stay on the Hawaiian Islands. Today, we are planning an extended tour throughout Europe.

This life didn't happen by accident. It was the result of substantial planning and work that began over 25 years ago. We shunned the illusion of luxury provided by popular consumer products and embraced the freedom that flows from financial independence.

You can also become financially independent in your own custom-built future if you choose. Your journey begins with a financial education and purposeful action steps. The first action step along your road to freedom is understanding what I have termed the **Tyrannical Rule of Money.** *This rule states that money is a requirement in everyone's life, and if you fail to control your money then your money will certainly control you.*

To understand this principle, let's start with the fact that everyone needs money to fund their lives. Even monks living in a monastery are supported by funds generated by their religious orders; or, the monks support themselves through the profits of various business enterprises.

Another example is the self-reliant mountain men of legend who lived beyond the edges of civilization. Mountain men also required money. They sold the furs they harvested from the wilderness for bullets, powder, and other essential supplies. The pioneers of old also needed money. Pioneers on the frontier traded crops and livestock for the money to purchase additional farm and household supplies. That is why pioneers were indebted to the local store owner when crops failed to produce a profit.

Occasionally, you hear about cult leaders who take their followers into the wilderness to escape society and the need for money. They always fail or end up learning they actually do require money to fund their lives. Communists also dreamed of ridding their socialist society from the evils of capitalistic money. Of course, the communists' attempts to rid themselves of money have never worked out for them—nor will it ever work out. This is because money exerts a constant force on everyone's life.

It does not matter whether you choose to honor the **Tyrannical Rule of Money,** ignore it, or don't believe in it. This rule remains an absolute fact. In other words, to keep from dancing to money's tune, you must understand how money works in your life.

Those who work to understand how money impacts virtually every aspect of their lives are the final winners. Those who make the effort to understand personal finance and basic investing always come out ahead. Once you understand that you will require money, both now and in your future, the quest simply becomes to control its power for your own ends rather than have it control you.

Most people require a constantly increasing influx of money to service growing debt and to pay for their daily lives. This can be true even if they have already earned a lot of money from past employment. Plenty of people finish a year, a decade, or even an entire career and still have no money. Other people go broke even though they are currently making huge amounts of money each week.

You only have to look at high-paid celebrities and athletes who go broke to understand that they failed to control their large incomes. Celebrities know a great deal about entertainment or athleticism, but they may know absolutely nothing about managing their money.

Lottery winners are also notorious for going broke. This is because simply giving someone money does nothing to help them master money's power in their life. Some lottery winners who were given large sums of money did not have the knowledge required to manage their new fortunes. If the lottery winners did not learn how to manage their money prior to winning, they will have no idea how to manage the significant power created by large sums of money landing in their bank accounts.

A working career of 25 to 35 years is a long time. Over such a long period of time, you could easily lose focus of your objective. I have found six concepts that will clarify for you the best strategy in a wage-based employment system to achieve your goals.

I call my six strategies **Financial Freedom Principles.** *The Financial Freedom Principles are big-picture concepts that will provide you with a clearer understanding of your overall lifelong strategy.* Some of these principles will be familiar to you, others probably will not. The ultimate purpose of these principles is, of course, to obtain freedom in your future.

Financial Freedom Principle #1: *The earlier you begin saving and investing your wages, the greater your opportunity to harness the power of money for your own desires.* You harness money's power through compounding interest. Your money, placed in appropriate retirement investments, begins generating additional money almost immediately.

That money (from compounding interest) is automatically rolled back into your account. You then earn interest (money) on your new, higher balance—and so on. Your goal with this process is to create a great machine that will generate an income stream for your use in the future.

I have seen this plan work for many people. In 1981, I started training in the police academy in Dayton, Ohio. As a young person, I had the energy, drive, ambition, and the illusion that I knew exactly what I was doing.

I met another young officer at the academy who sat directly in front of me during those endless classes on police procedures, state law, constitutional law, and report writing. Like me, he knew the value of goal setting and working hard to fulfill his dreams.

His financial goals, however, were significantly more ambitious than mine. He developed a plan to obtain the future he desired. First he believed in his heart that he could succeed and went on to achieve success through a set of simple action steps. The universe, as it often does, honored his request.

This young police recruit, from his very first paycheck in the academy, began putting away large portions of his salary into various retirement accounts. He continued to annually increase the dollar amount he invested by routing his pay raises and most of his overtime money into his investment accounts. To reach the goals he had set for himself, he gladly drove an old car, lived in a small house, and was much more frugal than most people.

I don't want to give you the impression that this young officer lived a monk-like existence, as he did not! He went out with his friends, had good times, and dated many different people. He simply enjoyed all those activities at the more moderate end of the scale.

This officer was a multimillionaire in about 23 years. Nothing much changed in his life when he achieved his goal. He continued living his life, working the same job until he retired a few years later, and continued living the life that he had chosen.

He now lives a relatively carefree life, traveling across the United States and abroad, still dating, and simply doing whatever suits him at the moment. Such a life can be yours if you are willing to work for it. Although my personal success in this area was no small accomplishment, it didn't come close to the financial freedom that this young man created for himself. This was truly an amazing accomplishment that I can only envy.

Some of the students in my financial freedom classes have exclaimed, "This is a ridiculous idea! I don't want to toil away in misery until I'm in my late fifties or sixties to become independent." "Terrific!" I always say. Please don't let me hold you up! Go create that successful business, produce that movie, write that book, and create whatever will make you independently rich. I applaud you for even trying to achieve success in this way.

Of course, I understand that is not what they really meant. What they really meant was that they were unwilling to sacrifice what they wanted in the present for a better tomorrow. "Fine with me!" I say. *We each have total responsibility for our life outcomes. If you don't work to create the future you want, then you get the future you deserve.*

Financial Freedom Principle #2: *Your work career has an expiration date, and your career clock is ticking right now!* Everyone knows that the average career life of a professional athlete is very short. The average NFL (National Football League) career, for example, is somewhere between three and seven years. At the end of their professional careers, many of these football players are broke. The average NBA (National Basketball Association) career runs only somewhere between four and 12 years. It is also not uncommon for an NBA player to be broke at the end of his career.

The career of a firefighter is more or less 25 years, due to the very strenuous and hazardous nature of that job. But what is the average career span of a plumber? A plumber cannot typically work at his profession until the day he dies. His job is physically strenuous and demanding. The same is true for police officers, electricians, delivery people, and a host of business professionals. Illnesses, injuries, and old age take their toll.

Since I worked in the police field, I know the average career of a police officer (if not severely injured performing his or her duties) is around 25 to 30 years. It is a short career, because a 60-year-old (or older) officer will not typically perform well in confrontations with 18-year-old, street-fit youths looking for trouble.

At the end of their careers, most officers have very little money saved and must move on to yet another job—even though they are collecting a moderate pension. Most police officers have earned a lot of money over their careers. In a larger department, an officer has typically earned between 1.5 and 2.5 million dollars. Some officers achieve financial security at the end; however, the vast majority do not.

No matter what your profession, as you age, you lose strength, become less physically agile, injure more easily, and heal much more slowly. How often have you heard people say they are on the "work-until-they-die-plan?" Working until the day you die is not actually a plan.

As you age, you slow down mentally and physically. Additionally, ageism is still very much alive and well in the workplace. You can expect to be downsized, rightsized and otherwise pushed out of higher paying jobs when you reach a certain age. On average, my research indicates older workers make less money for the same work done by younger employees.

Life-long income from wages can follow something of a curve (what I call the **Lifetime Earnings Arc).** Generally, at the start of your career, wages are lower. As you gain work experience, you gradually make more and more money. Your career and salary typically begin to peak in your mid-fifties to early sixties. By your mid to late sixties, you have peaked, and your earnings stagnate or tend to drop. Your working career (working for others for income) is limited so make the most of it.

The **Lifetime Earnings Arc** means that *you must also limit the amount of money you are spending.* Spending more than you make is not an option if you want freedom in the future. Reject the counterfeit happiness provided by material stuff around the house and embrace the true freedom that comes from financial independence.

Financial Freedom Principle #3: *You are essentially on your own in the future. In essence, you are working for yourself from the beginning of your work life.* The government may or may not use the Social Security money they removed from your pay check to benefit you in your old age. They are just as likely to use your money for totally unrelated purposes—and history has repeatedly demonstrated this to be a sad fact.

Social Security taxes have been used time and time again by our elected officials for purposes other than supplementing the income of retirees and older workers. Whether or not you're an advocate for the causes for which your Social Security money was re-appropriated is entirely irrelevant. The fact is that much of the money has already been spent and is not available to fund the retirements of our nation's elderly without a constant infusion of new cash.

Every drawback mentioned regarding Social Security applies to company pensions. Company pensions have been used for other purposes, confiscated, stolen, mismanaged by their boards, absorbed by other companies, or simply cancelled and used as operating capital by the companies who had control of the pension funds. The sad truth is, if it is not in your personal account, you may or may not receive payments from the funds you contributed.

Another trend working against older employees includes the downsizing of our work force due to increased technological efficiency. That means fewer employees pay into pension plans or our government's Social Security system. Most pension systems (including Social Security) rely upon payments from the current work force to fund them. Simply put, every dollar you earn is precious to you in the present and in your future.

Financial Freedom Principle #4: *Wealth can rarely be created for those who earn a low wage during their entire working career.* For this plan to succeed, you will need to make money—a lot of money. Your task is to figure out how to get better paying jobs and additional promotions. When that is done, you must obtain an even better paying job. An amazing future cannot be built on the foundation of minimum wage (or nearly minimum wage) jobs. There is certainly no shame starting in this category, you just can't finish your career in it.

Benjamin Franklin is one of our country's most distinguished founding fathers and also the father of building wealth in America. When Franklin was born, he was the fifteenth of seventeen children. His family was extremely poor. He began his working career as an apprentice in his brother's print shop at the age of 12.

His brother was extremely jealous of Franklin's obvious talents and kept him on a short leash. Benjamin soon illegally fled from his brother's apprentice position and started his own printing business in another city with the financial support of a few friends. His business became hugely successful.

Benjamin Franklin didn't stop with a single printing business. Franklin had unparalleled drive and ambition. His other successful businesses (that he started from scratch) included writing books, publishing, large-scale paper production, and a wholesale paper delivery system.

In the end, Franklin became one of the richest men of his time. He built a life that provided him the freedom he sought. Franklin wanted the freedom to live his life as he chose—not as others chose for him. Franklin rejected the rules imposed on him by his family, by poverty, and even by the English government in later years. He created his own path to riches and fame.

The lesson Benjamin Franklin provides us is that no one can achieve freedom and wealth by going with the flow or accepting the status quo. If Franklin had remained an apprentice with his brother, following the path he was required to follow by law, he would have had a very different life.

Reject the life that others live because it is conventional, easy, or comfortable. Reject buying expensive material possessions that give you a false sense of happiness and comfort. Instead, strive for excellence. Franklin walked his own path to achieve his amazing life.

Financial Freedom Principle #5: *Create multiple streams of income for your future.* This can be done a number of ways, depending on your personal preferences. It can include pension income, investment income, and business income. The more streams of income you are able to create for yourself, the more secure your financial future becomes.

Multiple streams of income also make you more financially resilient in hard times. Should one income stream die because of a changing economy, you have other income streams that will keep you from the gates of financial ruin—as long as your debt is not too high.

I met a couple that was retired and obviously living very well. As soon as I could, without causing them discomfort, I brought up the subject of money and investments. Amazingly, they knew nothing at all about the subject of investing.

The couple had created so many different streams of income for their family that it made investing almost irrelevant to them. The husband had worked for the railroad until he retired. He received a pension from that job. He also joined the army reserves. After 25 years of military reserve service to his country (including combat service), he received a second pension.

When he retired from the railroad, he began working as a railroad safety consultant. He is now working part-time in his own consulting business and has all the work he wants. His wife also is retired and receiving a pension from her teaching job. Recently, they became eligible for Social Security.

As you can see, investments are simply not a priority for them. I applaud the couple for planning ahead and utilizing all the options available to them to create the life they wanted. Nothing stops you from following a similar path.

Income stream creation, like all of these **Financial Freedom Principles,** has been used throughout our recorded history. Benjamin Franklin, mentioned earlier in this chapter, created multiple streams of income by writing, publishing, paper distribution, and running America's first post office.

George Washington's career is another excellent example of the power of creating multiple income streams. Many of the presidents died virtual paupers, such as Thomas Jefferson and James Monroe. Washington, however, died a very wealthy man.

He started creating income streams as a young man when he became a land surveyor on the frontier. He immediately began investing his money in land—essentially becoming a land speculator. Later, he made a fortune in farming, commercial fishing, and distribution of commercial fish products throughout the East. He also owned a commercial distillery. The money Washington made far overshadowed any money he or his wife inherited. When his money is adjusted for inflation, Washington is considered the richest president in American history.

Most people, of course, do not work for the government and will not receive a government pension when they retire. That does not put them out of the multiple income stream race. I have known many people who have started their own small businesses in their spare time to create separate income streams from their regular employment.

You need not be the next Mark Zuckerberg, with the next big tech idea, to successfully create a start-up business. Plenty of no-tech to low-tech small businesses perform terrifically and create income streams for their owners—like washing windows for example. Creating a business from scratch also teaches you new skills and provides you with additional business experience. This, in turn, makes you more marketable and more versatile in the future.

Creating an additional stream of income from the real estate market is now very popular. I totally support this idea, with the forewarning that it is much more difficult than it seems. Don't be fooled by the seminar gurus who make it sound virtually effortless. When a profit is realized by a real estate investor, it typically occurs only after the sale of the property.

There are many hidden costs and expenses that novice real estate investors may initially fail to realize. A police officer I know became wealthy through real estate investing. He purchased and maintained rental properties. He says that market research in the area of interest is one of the keys to success. He also admitted that he suffered through several years of hard knocks before he understood how to make money with real estate.

One of the best ideas for success in real estate investing, or in any other business, is to find a mentor. Find someone who is already successful, someone who has already made the journey you now want to make. Take them to lunch and ask them questions. Most people are flattered and happy to share their experiences with you. Also, becoming an apprentice is one of the best ways to learn a new business. Some businesses will allow you to work in their company to learn the industry—as long as they have assurances that you won't be a direct competitor later.

Financial Freedom Principle # 6: *The basic goal of saving your money today is to create a nest egg that generates income in your future.* Principle #6 builds upon Financial Freedom Principle #5, which stresses the generation of income streams.

Let's say you work at saving diligently for 30 years and you eventually amass a sizable nest egg—called your principle. When the time comes to leave your job, you do not use the money you have saved (principle). Instead, your plan will be to utilize the income your nest egg generates (passive investment income) for your new life. If you do this, the money will continue to produce an income stream for you throughout your life. However, when you omit this principle, it drastically reduces your income stream.

Your future success in earning money as an employee is totally dependent upon your ability to turn your wages into a passive income stream for your future use. Let me emphasize it again, converting your wages into passive investment income will be one of the largest determinants of your freedom later in life. Although this plan may not be very sexy in the present, trust me that it radiates sex appeal a little later!

Your goal, with the money you converted from your wages, is to essentially build a money machine that will outlive you. Sometimes your money machine creates a lot of income. Sometimes it makes a little less income. Sometimes it even falters or stops creating income for a bit.

You can smooth out these rough spots by withdrawing a lower percentage of your money, on average, than your money earns. Your ultimate financial goal is to build, and then preserve, diverse income streams. Passive income (requiring little work or effort from you on a daily basis) from investments is one of the primary vehicles open to everyone.

Creating a money machine is not a simple academic exercise. Instead, it is an undertaking that could likely be your ticket to future freedom. Consider that a million dollars has the power to generate quite a bit of income. For example, 5% interest on a million dollars is 50,000 a year (these are examples, not guaranteed returns, based upon investment type, interest rates, the current economy, etc.).

This money comes in even if you sleep late and never work again. Your money never gets sick, never takes a day off, and never quits. It just keeps earning income for your later use. Now that we have discussed one million dollars, let's talk about having some real money.

What if you had two million dollars in an account—not at all an insurmountable amount to amass during a working career? Now we are talking $100,000 a year in income on your 5% earnings. Again, you now need only to manage your investments, live a reasonable lifestyle, and live your life as you choose—within the bounds of a budget and financial common sense.

TO: Present You
FROM: Future You
SUBJECT: Message from Your Future #5

Hello:

A job is first and foremost about earning money from your labor. Period! There is no other reason to have a job if it is not to earn money to fund your life. If the point of a job is not about the money you earn, but is instead about an altruistic goal, then it would be called volunteering! Some people object to this view and repeat the often-used axiom that money is not everything. Some people claim that other factors in your job are just as important—such as helping people.

It is true that money isn't everything. Nonetheless, can you afford a 50% pay cut in your current position and still be fiscally sound? Can you quit your job and be fine? Chances are, you cannot afford that kind of income reduction. This exercise crystalizes for you (I would certainly hope) that jobs are about income. Next in line are concerns about tolerating your prevailing job conditions. The third concern is actually about altruism or a dedication to the cause of your profession.

Money is important in everyone's life. Reject those who would have you believe that money is not important. Poverty creates soul-shattering misery and restricts your freedom of choice. Most of us have the wonderful option to choose not to be poor! Choosing prosperity is a much better idea for you and your loved ones. Money is involved in virtually every aspect of your life, whether you realize it or not. The **Tyrannical Rule of Money** states that *money is a requirement in everyone's life and if you fail to control your money, then your money will certainly control you.*

With a job, you have the opportunity (some would say the obligation) to save for your future. The point of this saving is to create a passive income stream for later in life—not to spend the principle amount that creates the income stream. The more income streams you create for yourself in the future, the more resilient your income and lifestyle will be.

The **Financial Freedom Principles** below will help you create a financially abundant life if you heed them:

- The earlier you begin saving and investing, the more money will be available to you in the future.

- Don't think that you can work forever. You cannot! Your work career and work life is limited. Don't waste the time you have by failing to save the money you earn through your labors.

- You are on your own. Don't expect the government, your family, or anyone else to do for you what you should be doing for yourself.

- Work to maximize your income through promotions, better jobs, upgrading your work skills, starting a business on the side, or any other technique that suits your abilities, interests, and skill sets.

- Create multiple streams of income for your use in the future. Create income streams through pensions, investments, business creation, or any other means that appeal to you. The more income streams you have, the more resilient your future will be.

- One reason to have a job is to save your wages in order to create an income stream later in your life. You use your nest egg to create this income stream. You should only use the income created from your nest egg and never the nest egg itself. If you forget this principle, you will literally kill your goose that is laying your golden eggs!

GROWTH

Six

Control Your Income

We all have dreams. But in order to make dreams come into reality, it takes an awful lot of determination, dedication, self-discipline, and effort.

— Jesse Owens

As a young man, I sat in the living room of my friend's house in one of his overstuffed chairs. We were having a beer and pondering life's many mysteries. One of the greatest mysteries was our retirement savings plans. I had been on the police department for a few years. My friend was also an officer for the same city and had been in his job for a bit longer. He and I were examining our retirement savings balances as we sipped our beers.

We both had the goal of creating million-dollar account balances before we retired. As we looked at my balance and how much I was saving each month, his concern grew. "You are not going to make it," my friend told me. "There is simply no way you can save a million dollars at this rate!" I had to admit that he seemed to have a point. "You could be right," I said glumly. I was putting away as much as I could afford, which was about $150 a month at that time. I seemed to be a thousand miles away from my goal.

How could I possibly achieve my goal at this rate? This conversation spurred me to do some more research. At 7%

interest, not unusual at that time, it would take about $850 a month for 30 years to obtain a million dollars in my retirement accounts. My projected balance was nowhere near this amount. It appeared my friend was right. I was not going to achieve this goal. The problem appeared to be an unscalable mountain.

Creating abundant financial resources is one of the cornerstones of an amazing life. Abundant financial resources allow you the luxury to choose your own future. Without income to fund your life in the future, you create a life in which your options are severely limited. However, with freedom and options in life, it is easier to pursue your own particular brand of happiness.

The road to an amazing life, however, must be taken one step at a time. *Two important steps are necessary to achieving financial abundance:*

- Incrementally increasing your savings over your working lifetime.

- Controlling your spending.

Most people could empathize with the problem with which I struggled so many years ago. I could not afford to put away enough money (seemingly) to achieve my million-dollar savings goal! I have since learned that the road to my goal is not a static process.

We all have what I have termed a **Lifetime Savings Arc.** This is my phrase to describe a family's or individual's ability to earn more and more money as they age. In the beginning, when wages are low, a family can only save a small amount of their income. As the family ages and the family's work situations improve, their income increases in comparison to their beginning wages. As your income increases, the opportunity to save more money also increases.

My wife and I learned later that we only contributed a little more than 1/3 of the total financial balance that we enjoy today.

The forces of money, time, and compounding interest contributed the rest of the funds for us. The investment balances grew exponentially as a result of the returns on our investments. Compounding interest, more than anything else, helped us to achieve our goals. *Albert Einstein called compounding interest the most powerful force in the universe. It is easy to see why.*

What this means to you is that you don't have to contribute a million dollars to obtain this amount in your account. For example, if you had $300,000, and left it in the bank for twenty-five years, at a rate of about 5% interest, a million dollars could easily be yours. The trick is the speed at which you can put your portion of money into the bank so that it can begin to earn interest to fund your future. The earlier, and the more you can contribute, the more money you will have.

I agree that most people can't contribute a huge sum like $300,000 right away. The strategy, therefore, is to make up for this initial savings deficit by contributing more and more money to your investment accounts each year. A program of continuous savings works like a ladder, with the lowest rung of the ladder being the amount you save in your early working years.

Each year, you save more and more. An easy way to lessen this pain is to make more money each year. That way, you don't feel the bite of the plan as much as you would with a constant income. This is why increasing your annual income is critically important and occupies a large portion of this text.

The use of payroll deductions to route pre-taxed money directly to our retirement accounts was a significant step in this process for me. Uncle Sam is cut out of the equation (at least temporarily), and you use pre-taxed dollars. That means that if you are in the 25% tax bracket, for every dollar you put into a tax deferred retirement account, you are paying .25 cents less in tax that year. That also means you get the benefit of the entire dollar growing in your account, rather than just the .75 cents you would have received after taxes.

Moreover, for every $100 dollars you save in a retirement account, you get the benefit of an extra $25 to grow on your own behalf. In essence, you keep more of the money you make. This is a good deal for Uncle Sam as well. In the future, our favorite uncle gets his fair share when you withdraw some of the money from your retirement accounts.

Most companies now provide at least some matching funds if you will utilize a retirement savings plan that the company officially authorizes—typically a 401K plan. A 401K plan is simply a tax-deferred savings plan authorized by the Internal Revenue Service.

Failing to take advantage of this benefit is like giving your employer a refund on the wages they pay you. There is absolutely no reason not to take full advantage of this additional money from your employer.

As a side note, my wife and I have learned from experience that many employer-sponsored retirement accounts are riddled with fees, which are sometimes hidden! Your employer's specific retirement savings account (usually 401K) fees are something you will have to research and become familiar with. Nevertheless, these fees should not deter your use of the retirement savings plan. When you change employers you can roll this money out of your employer's fee-ridden 401K plan to a plan of your choice—such as a Vanguard account or a Fidelity account, with lower fees.

Additionally, the U.S. Supreme Court ruled just this year in the **Tibble v. Edison** case that employers have a "fiduciary responsibility" to monitor their sponsored 401K plans and offer appropriate choices to their employees. In other words, employers must offer 401K plans with fees that are reasonable and a plan that is appropriate.

You should research your employer's plan, its accompanying fees, and this recent court decision. You may have to work with your employer to improve your 401K plan choices. Most employers are willing to listen to employees' concerns in this area. After all, management personnel utilize these same plans. If it's a bad deal for you, it is also a bad deal for them.

Many people argue that a Roth retirement account is a much better idea. A Roth account utilizes after-tax money to save for your retirement. In other words, you pay into the account with money Uncle Sam has already taxed. The government, in turn, does not tax you on the earnings your investments have generated. Consequently, all withdrawals are tax free at the proper age.

My research indicates that, once the tax liability for both types of accounts is considered, as it corresponds to a 30-year time frame, there is little difference between the two types of accounts. Which type of account you should choose depends upon when you want to lower your tax liability—now or in your future? In some cases, taxes may not be an issue for you in the present.

Some people attempt to save primarily on their own, without using a payroll deduction plan. In my experience, this strategy is rarely successful. The household money, designated for retirement savings, inevitably ends up being hijacked for something else—much like what has happened to our government-controlled Social Security System. This type of yo-yo budgeting creates boom and bust cycles in your family's financial and personal lives. Yo-yo budgeting impedes the saving commitments you must make to be successful. If the money enters your retirement account before you ever receive your paycheck, it makes the entire savings process easier.

I freely admit that 25 to 30 years does seem like quite a long time to save. If you are determined not to wait, I totally understand your impatience. Your future self is impatient as well and wants prosperity to come your way as quickly as possible. If you want wealth to accumulate sooner, then you need to develop a more aggressive plan. Decide upon your goals, develop the appropriate strategy, and get started today! Any plan of this sort will involve sacrifice and work.

Jesse Owens was certainly no stranger to sacrifice in order to achieve his goals. He was born on September 12, 1913, to poor parents who were sharecroppers in Danville, Alabama. He was the seventh child born into this impoverished family in the Deep South. During his childhood, money and food were always in short supply.

His family moved to Cleveland, Ohio, seeking a better life. In Cleveland, a track coach recognized his natural talent and began to train him. Yet his training was no less important to him than helping his family survive. Throughout high school, Owens worked a part-time job to help support his struggling family.

When Owens was recruited by Ohio State's track program, the university helped find his dad a job to support the large Owens family. Jesse worked three jobs throughout college and still managed to keep up with his studies and his track and field work. He scarified continually to obtain his goals.

Jesse Owens' athletic career culminated in the 1936 Olympics in Berlin, Germany. At that time, Germany was controlled by the Nazis who believed that the Aryan race was physically superior to all others. Young Owens, an African American, trounced the Nazis in track and field and won four gold medals. Owens' victories were an amazing feat that remained unequaled in Olympic history for 50 years.

The sacrifices made by Owens and his family to obtain his amazing life were inspiring. Even though he continued to have money issues, stemming from the lack of opportunity brought on by the rampant racism of that age, his accomplishments remain nothing short of astonishing. Although he did not die wealthy, he was certainly much better off than he would have been without the vision of his future that he was determined to create. All of my sacrifices, and probably yours as well, pale in comparison to the ones made by this young man and his family. Owens created his own amazing life from virtually nothing.

The **Tyrannical Rule of Money** states that you must control your money or your money will certainly control you. Money does not care about you in any conceivable way! It flows through your life and its power is inescapable. Control your money's power or become its slave. These are your only two choices in life. *I offer three steps to become your money's master, to control its power, and to force it to do your bidding.*

Step one: Complete a budget. Yes, I already know you hate budgeting. You will hate economic ruin much more than you hate budgeting—trust me on that! If it's any consolation, I don't like budgeting tasks any better than you do. Luckily for me, however, my lovely wife doesn't absolutely detest it—but certainly has no love for it either. You must know how much money is coming in to fund your current lifestyle. Without this knowledge, it is impossible to gain control over your money, leaving you open to money's cruel tyranny.

Step two: Control your daily spending. It is very easy to outspend your available budget. Famous celebrities, doctors, lawyers, CEOs, and others go broke every year by spending more than they make. In fact, spending more than you make has become the cultural norm. This norm will deny you freedom in the future. Purchases of luxury items in the present gives you the illusion of luxury and abundance. In reality, they represent the chains of bondage that rob you of your future.

Once your needs are reasonably met, material possessions will not make you happier. At a certain point, good is simply good enough. This is not to say that I don't desire more. Yes, I want more cars, better houses, yachts, and more of everything else—except more women. Mrs. Faulkner has clearly explained to me that more women are something I do not want—and why I don't want them!

This brings us to the old adage, "You can have anything you want, just not everything you want." The trick is to get control of your own personal desire monster. The desire monster we each carry with us insists that you will only be happy if you shun the economy car and buy a Mercedes. It's the monster that convinces you that a small house won't do. You, being special, obviously need to live in a huge house on a large estate. It is the monster that tells you that you must have a vacation home, rather than stay at a hotel to finally be happy. The monster lies to us and is the enemy of freedom.

Step three: Avoid creating risk to your future by creating excessive debt. Debt creates financial risk in your future. A job loss due to an economic downturn, a significant injury, or a serious illness, has the potential to create financial ruin. If a mishap occurs, even through no fault of your own, you could find yourself unable to service your large debt obligations. Every debt you take on is a risk. Sometimes, debt is good, but most of the time it is not.

As a result of the economic downturn that began in 2007, thousands of people lost their jobs in 2008–2009. Because of the downturn, jobs were suddenly in short supply. The problem was that our cultural norm was to live just at, or even beyond, our means.

Consequently, many were unable to service their massive debt during the economic downturn. This led to defaults on their loans and home mortgages. Many of our neighbors had debt so high that they could not possibly take less money in another job—even if they could find another job. Rid yourself of all the debt that you can, which will reduce the financial risk to your future.

Here is an illustration of how this works in your life. Consider the typical adult toy purchases. Many people like motorcycles, while other people favor nice ski boats. Both are certainly a lot of fun. Everybody who has a good job and works hard deserves a motorcycle or a boat after all.

Besides, motorcycles save us money on gas in the long run, while we can use the boat with the entire family on weekends. After looking at our budget, we decide we can comfortably utilize $20,000 in wages (paid in monthly installments) to make this purchase. Let's even say we get a super deal of 4% percent financing, sponsored by the manufacturer for five years. What a great deal!

Adult Toy of Choice:

- $20,000 Cost
- 0% Down
- 4% Manufacturer Sponsored Finance Charge
- 5-Year Term
- $368.00 Monthly Payment for 5 Years

Total principle and interest paid on this loan is $22,099—that's not bad at all!

If we wanted to rescue our unhappy, message-sending future self, we might decide on a slightly different plan. Instead, you open an IRA (Individual Retirement Account) or a 401K (a tax deferred retirement account) and deposit this same amount into your account by using payroll deduction. Let's say you earn about the same amount of return on your money and at the end of five years (the following paragraphs are simply examples and not guaranteed returns) you now possess $22,098 instead of a motorcycle or a boat.

Chances are, when you consider the price, you might still rather have the motorcycle or weekends with the family on your new boat. However, what if you left that same money alone in that same IRA or 401K, without adding or subtracting any cash? If you did that, you now possess $58,912 using the same 4% interest premise in 25 years. Perhaps this plan is beginning to garner a little more interest for you.

I believe you can probably do much better with your investments. If you used a balanced portfolio strategy (balanced between bonds and stock mutual funds, let's say) you could receive something in the neighborhood of 6 to 7% interest annually (see Chapter 7).

This is a historical calculation that is more or less accurate when a long-term average is calculated. At the end of the same 25 years, using the same $22,000 total, without adding even another dime to the account, you now have approximately $119,940 in your account. This is approaching the edge of some life changing money.

Boats, motorcycles, large homes, vacation homes, RVs, horses for leisure, and expensive collections are the enemy of your future. These types of purchases leverage your future income and make those funds unavailable for retirement savings. Instead of buying these things, consider short-term rentals when you have the need and time to enjoy them. Although that is still an expensive proposition, it is much more cost effective than paying for these consumer products year round, regardless of whether you actually use them or not.

The above section is a brief introduction to the concept of **opportunity costs from the science of macroeconomics. The term opportunity cost is a phrase used to describe the economic consequences or costs of favoring one choice over another.** In the above scenario, embracing the cost of a motorcycle or boat implies that you are willing to forgo the opportunity to invest the same money in an attempt to create income in your future.

A series of choices that favor your present over your future prosperity will likely mean that you are severely limiting your future. In other words, you would be violating Rule #7 for Life Success that reminds us that our actions today significantly impact our future.

Not all choices are as clear cut as the motorcycle purchase. For example, many of you have accumulated debt in an attempt to create a more abundant future. In other words, you have decided to accumulate student loan debt now in exchange for an education that you believe will increase your prosperity in both the present and the future.

The problem you are now experiencing, however, is that your current student loan debt significantly impacts your ability to save your wages and therefore, hampers your effort to create income for your future self. Student loan debt also increases your present financial risks over the period of time you carry that debt.

To create the future you envision, student loan debt needs to be dealt with aggressively. Only five possible options exist to handle student debt:

- Pay the school loan off in the agreed time period before saving money for your retirement or your financial freedom plan.

- Implement a blended plan of debt repayment and saving for your future financial freedom.

- Pay off your debt in half the allotted time and then save for your financial freedom.

- Find an employer who will pay your college debt for you while you save for your financial freedom.

Simple math will go a long way in guiding you in choosing the correct strategy. In the analysis below, we will make the assumption you have $36,800 in school debt and a payment of $364 a month for 10 years. For the sake of consistency, we will say that you could also earn 6% annually on money you invest for your master plan to achieve your own personal financial freedom (utilizing a balanced portfolio of equities, bonds, etc. that emphasizes a strategy of index tracking explained in chapters 7 & 8).

The exact interest rate you earn is not as important as using the same number for all your comparisons. We will also assume you have a work career (with an accompanying working life expectancy) of about 30 years **(see Financial Freedom Principle #2)**. All the investment savings figures in these comparisons were made by using a compound interest calculator at investor.gov.

In **Strategy 1,** you pay off your loan in 10 years, as initially scheduled. After you pay off your student loan, you roll this payment into your investment plans to achieve your financial freedom in the future. After 20 years of saving this amount monthly, you would only have $160,883.

The amount is low (especially when considering your 30 years of labor), because you robbed yourself of the critical savings period (the first 10 years) that occurred at the beginning of your working career. This is sad, because had you saved this same $364 from the beginning of your working career, you would have obtained a balance of over twice this amount—coming in at around $345,332 ($364 a month for 30 years at 6% interest compounded annually).

Strategy 2 is a plan in which you save a little money and also pay off the loan debt as initially scheduled. You also save $100 a month until your student loan is paid off in 10 years, and then you pay $364 a month into your investment accounts. In this course of action, you do a little better than your previous attempt. You come in at around $211,413 after 30 years of labor. This is a little better, but by no means your best course of action.

In **Strategy 3,** you buckle down and pay off your student loan debt in only five years. This leaves you 25 years of uninterrupted investing. This is very doable, as people pay off new car loans with similar balances in five years' time. You then roll your entire student loan payment into your financial freedom's savings plan. At the end of 25 years, you have about

$239,652 (the actual amount would be slightly larger due to a decrease in interest charges because of your early payoff).

The only better option than cutting your payment period by half is not to accumulate any student debt in the first place. *Obviously, the higher the student debt, or the higher the interest rate on your loan, the more important this strategy becomes to your present and future.*

Besides pointing out the best student loan management strategy, this is a stark lesson for those who fail to save for their financial freedom until they are older.

The first 10 years of work is one of the most critical periods for wealth accumulation. Failing to save during this period could easily reduce your lifetime savings balance by more than half (see **Financial Freedom Principle #1).**

The outcomes of the strategies to pay off school debt and save for your future (given a work career of 30 years):

- **Strategy 1:** Paying off school debt in the allotted 10 years before saving any money for your future financial freedom = **$160,883.**

- **Strategy 2:** Implementing a blended plan of paying $100/month into investments, paying off your debt in the allotted ten years, and afterwards, making a $364/month payment into your investment for 20 years = **$211,413.**

- **Strategy 3:** Paying off school debt in 5 years and then saving the $364/month for your financial freedom = **$239,652.**

This now leaves **Strategy 4,** which is to get your employer to pay your student loan debt. This is always a good plan if you can manage it. If you can find an employer that is willing to make the payments for you, then you have effectively cancelled your student loan debt. This leaves you free to save for your future financial freedom as your employer services your student loans.

Some Federal Government jobs will pay a portion of your college debt. The FBI, for example, pays on their agents' student loan debt under certain conditions. If you join the armed forces, they will also pay a *portion* of your debt, as will the military reserves. Other companies will make your student loan debt payment a bonus for remaining with the company for a set period of time—typically three or more years. Finally, you can clear the loan balance on some federal student loans by working in an underserved area, like an Indian reservation, for a preset period of time.

Most of your friends, of course, will not deal aggressively with their debt. Most of your friends will not implement a system to automatically deposit their paychecks into tax deferred retirement accounts—or may only use this system very modestly. Most people get the consumer product they want right away. Most people spend all the money they earn from their wage-based jobs.

If you do these things, too, you are being consistent with your peer group. Of course, you will also achieve the same outcome your peers will experience. To create a different outcome, you must get acquainted with sacrificing today for a more abundant future tomorrow. Those who are able to sacrifice in the present to obtain amazing futures are the clear winners.

TO: Present You
FROM: Future You
SUBJECT: Message from Your Future #6

Hello again:

I am urging you to immediately begin using a payroll deduction plan to fund your IRA or 401K retirement savings plan. Payroll deduction offers the simplest way to accomplish your goal of building abundance. You have the potential to accomplish so much, but only if you will commit to your goals.

If you try to budget and save on your own, you are likely to get into boom-and-bust cycles of household finance, called yo-yo budgeting. Yo-yo budgeting will leave you little to show for all your hard work. A much easier way, a much more successful way, is to use payroll deduction to fund your retirement accounts. Using this method, you have little opportunity to spend the money on luxury items.

Starting a payroll deduction plan is just the beginning. The next steps include controlling your spending, keeping your overall debt burden low, and continually increasing your savings muscle by incrementally escalating your savings.

Aggressively handle your school debt. The best option (behind not accumulating school debt in the first place) is to find an employer who will pay your school debt for you. The next best option is to pay off your school debt in half the time and then roll that payment into your savings plan.

Please don't get discouraged. The key is to persevere over time. Keep putting raises and other salary increases into your investment/retirement funds. This is the road to obtaining your own amazing future.

MONEY FLOW

SEVEN

Diversity is the Spice of Life

I buy when other people are selling.

— J. Paul Getty

In 2012, I had lunch with a friend who was a successful doctor in the Dayton, Ohio region. We had known each other for years. The doctor was well known in our community, had a large family, a large house, sent his kids to private schools, and always drove a very nice luxury vehicle. He had several offices in the surrounding suburbs of Dayton and was seemingly successful and smart.

As we sat and talked, he turned our conversation to money. This was not a typical lunch conversation for the good doctor, so the conversation immediately piqued my interest. "Are you in the market?" he asked me. "My guy says the market (financial market) is going to drop big time," he said as he looked at me expectantly. "Yes, I am in the market," I replied. "Well, you need to get out!" he retorted abruptly. "My guy says a big market crash is coming very soon." It was quite obvious that he totally believed his unnamed guy's advice, which I assume was some sort of financial professional.

"Crap," I thought to myself. Advice like he had just repeated to me probably indicated the good doctor was listening to an advisor who either did not have his best interests in mind, or had no idea what he or she was talking about. In my opinion, his advisor was not helping him at all. As a side note, almost unrelated to this point, three years later after our conversation, the market has not yet crashed and has continued going up substantially.

"It's not really about what the market is going to do tomorrow or in the next few months," I tell him. "The important thing is, do you like your overall asset portfolio mix? You either like your asset allocation mix or you don't." As I began to explain just a little more, I saw him look past me into the great void. I could tell by his eyes that he had totally lost interest in the words coming out of my mouth! He was thinking about something else. "Blah, blah, blah," was all he was hearing from me. I simply changed the topic.

From his perspective, there was probably no reason not to tune me out. An investment professional, one that he was undoubtedly paying handsomely through commissions and fees, was giving him advice to immediately exit the equity (stock) financial markets. I, on the other hand, was just a cop.

If he had stayed focused on our conversation just a bit longer, I could have shown him the beginning of a path that would have significantly improved his chances to obtain the financial future he actually desired—rather than a future of limited resources he seemed destined to achieve.

The doctor was absolutely right in only one respect—the market will go down! It will go down and likely stay down for several years—except when it doesn't. Then, the market will go up. The market will likely go up and probably stay up for several years—except when it doesn't.

The image of a financial professional who knows where the market is going in the short term is simply a load of cow manure. The myth is propagated by some financial product salespeople who have a vested interest in convincing you that they know where the market is headed so they can sell you investments that provide them with sales commissions or fees.

They can sell you financial investments to combat the coming downturn; or, sell you investments that maximize a pending upturn that is just around the corner. Finally, they will happily manage all your investments for a fee. Occasionally, some professionals are right and sometimes they are wrong. However, they do not know any more than you do about the financial market's direction in the short term. As hard as that is to believe, this is an absolute fact.

Disclaimer: This is a good time to discuss my qualifications to advise you regarding investment strategies. I have zero formal credentials that qualify me to advise you regarding your own financial investments. I don't have a single certification designated by professional financial sales organizations (which I actually now know to be a good thing). I have no fiduciary responsibility to do anything that is in your best interest now or in the future. You should never follow a single investment strategy I discuss unless you independently verify it through your own research and find it sound.

Encouraging independent study, after all, is the very point of this writing! Finally, I want to advise you that even if you do everything mentioned in my writings, it could yield different results for you depending upon your ability, economic trends, and other factors as yet unknown.

I can only say that the strategies I explain here are the concepts I learned during my own research and practiced in my own financial life. Many financially successful people that I know use these same concepts as well.

The long-term direction (10 to 20 years from now) of the market is up. It is driven up by inflation if nothing else. The short-term direction of the market, however, remains unknowable. By short term, I mean the direction of the market somewhere in the neighborhood of one to three or maybe four years. To even attempt to predict where the financial market is headed in the short term, you would have to possess an intimate knowledge of numerous issues including:

- Federal Reserve short-term direction and their future actions to guide our economy,

- The science of economics as it specifically relates to current U.S. economic conditions and Federal Reserve actions,

- Imminent geopolitical events,

- An intimate knowledge of the world's various economies and their immediate impact on our own economy,

- The ability to predict what investors will do tomorrow through a doctorate in financial markets/investor psychology,

- Looming severe weather or manmade disasters that will happen in both the U.S. or around the world in the near future,

- How the business cycle will play out and the cycle's impact upon company profitability and the financial markets, and

- Pending large-scale business scandals, or outright fraud, that will be uncovered, reported, and impact market directions.

Obviously, it would be impossible for one person to know all these things. It is even impossible for one person to know everything about just one of these subjects. No one, for example, could know in advance all of the geopolitical events that will impact the market in the short term.

It is certainly impossible to understand how all world economic events will impact the financial market. It is also impossible for anyone to fully understand investor psychology and what investors are likely to do in the immediate future. In other words, the short-term direction of the financial markets is unknowable.

Neither a financial sales professional, nor an individual who believes that they are very smart, can predict the market's direction tomorrow. Luckily, we don't really need to know any of these things to be extremely successful in managing our money to create our own amazing future.

In 1973, Princeton economist Burton Gordon Malkiel wrote his famous book, A Random Walk Down Wall Street. Have you heard about it? No! Of course you haven't, because it is not in the best interests of certain financial professionals to tell you about his work.

It is a famous work that proves its conclusion through use of historical, statistical data. In this book, Malkiel used market data to prove that no one (emphasis on no one) can consistently predict the direction of stocks. No one can predict which stocks will prosper and which stocks will falter— without insider information.

His detailed analysis of data proved financial advisors/ sales professionals (those who are suggesting you should buy this or that because the market is going up or down) do not know any more than you or me. In fact, he believed that you would be better off throwing darts randomly at a stock chart on the wall (he actually suggested a monkey do this job) to pick stocks rather than listening to an investment professional who believes or pretends that he or she can pick stocks that will be winners and losers in the near future.

Never think that just because a person has a lot of formal education that they are knowledgeable about money, investing, or the financial market's short-term direction. This is true even if they are a rocket scientist, engineer, doctor, surgeon, or police chief. I have known people from each of these professions. Their money knowledge varied from knowing a great deal about the subject to knowing virtually nothing. Money management is not typically covered in a professional or academic education.

I hope you now agree with me that you can't control or even know the direction of the market in the short term. You can't control our U.S. economy. You can't control which stocks will do well. You cannot control current or foreign economic conditions. There are only a few things we, as individuals, can control in investing. Therefore, logic would dictate that you and I should concentrate our energies on the following issues:

- A balanced investment portfolio approach (based upon your risk tolerance) to increase investment safety and your long-term return on your investments,

- The utilization of index fund investing as your primary investment vehicle to increase investor safety and obtain the lowest possible fees,

- Keeping all investment fees as low as possible, and

- Minimizing taxes (not an issue if you use a pre-tax retirement account deducted from your paycheck or a Roth account)

I don't pretend to be smart enough to have thought of these concepts. I am only smart enough to have researched these issues on my own so that I am not confused by people who would take advantage of me—or be unduly influenced by people who have a faulty understanding of how investing really works. I encourage you to be this smart as well.

I learned about the importance of obtaining a financial education the hard way. My lack of financial knowledge knocked the wind out of my sails during the historical tech stock bubble of the early1990s. This was an exciting time in our history. It was the dawn of a new age, ushered in by the internet and affordable home computing.

Affordable computers, the internet, and the ability for consumers to use the internet to purchase almost anything, began a fundamental transformation of our economy. Companies began to form around these new technological advances. The new companies, even though few of them actually made money in the 1990s, became the "in thing."

Everyone understood that our economy had changed and was never going back to the way it was. Everyone rushed in to buy these new high-tech stocks they felt would lead the way into our "new economy." The value of the tech stocks rose quickly in anticipation of these companies making tons of money in the not-too-distant future. Few of these companies, however, were making any significant profit during this period.

From 1996 to 1999, the NASDAQ (a listing that emphasizes technology-based firms) sprinted unbelievably upward, from about 600 to just over the 5,000 mark (index is determined by a complicated formula involving weighted values determined by adding the value of all companies in the index and dividing by the number and size of the companies in the index).

I understood these historical and financial factors only minimally at the time. I simply bought the funds available in my 403b tax deferred retirement plan (named from the Internal Revenue Code that established it) that offered me the highest returns.

All the money I had saved was invested in only two funds. Although I knew the mutual funds I had purchased were invested in tech stocks, I did not understand how heavily they were invested in this area to increase the fund's profitability. I failed to understand that my investment decisions have real consequences in my future.

Rule for Life Success #7, states that *your actions today significantly impact your future.* I had invested in two funds that had an identical investment strategy. I was not familiar with the important concepts of *diversification or a balanced portfolio.* In short, I kept too many of my eggs in one basket.

The NASDAQ suddenly and drastically fell. The bubble burst and the pop was heard around the world! This was an unsustainable bubble, as opposed to a normal market downturn—which means the prices for high-tech stocks had left the realm of reality and grew until they simply exploded. My investments fell like a stone—all my investments. My loss was a staggering $100,000 in a relatively short period of time. To continue the basket analogy, someone kicked my basket across the room, and then stomped on it.

The **Tyrannical Rule of Money** came to my home and slapped me hard! My money dramatically controlled me, because I failed to control its power. I was emotionally devastated by this loss. I had foolishly lost a lot of money.

The problem I faced at the time was that the amount of money I had saved had outrun my knowledge of how to properly manage it. I had depended upon the professionals—active money managers in these mutual funds—to know which stocks to buy and which direction the market was going. This was a serious mistake.

At the beginning of your investment journey, you only need a little knowledge—such as, save early and invest the money you save. As your balance grows, your knowledge must grow with your balance. I began a course of study after this painful lesson.

I cannot possibly provide you with all the education you will need for investing. Instead, I want to point out the most important investment concepts I have learned and then send you forth on your own journey of discovery and self-study. This is a journey that cannot be completed in a day or a month, as it is always ongoing.

One of the key concepts I learned during my research was that Harry Markowitz and William Sharpe determined over two decades ago that if you own a balance of asset classes, it both increases your investments' safety and typically increases your financial returns (over an extended period of time).

By a balance, I mean a mix of equities (stocks which represent company ownership) and fixed investments (like bonds or annuity investments). A balanced portfolio means you are choosing asset classes (cash, stocks, bonds, annuities) that do not move in tandem (or in correlation) with each other. When one asset class goes down, some of your other asset classes are probably going up—more or less. This strategy acts as a parachute to slow any sudden drops—a strategy that has been proven to increase your returns over the long run.

It was Harry Markowitz and William Sharpe who learned that investing in this way made more money over the long haul, because it evens out the dramatic ups and downs of the financial markets. It is the dramatic ups and downs that slow your progress toward your financial goals. Their work is now the basis of modern portfolio theory and is now considered basic investing knowledge. Markowitz and Sharpe were awarded the Nobel Prize for Economics in 1990 for their development of modern portfolio theory.

This means that you, as an investor, should choose a mix of investments you are comfortable with and maintain that mix. For example, my wife and I have chosen an asset mix that includes 55% in fixed (bonds or annuity) funds, while 45% of our investments are in equity (stock) index funds. We typically maintain this overall balance.

That means if the bottom drops out of the equity market, and stocks go down 50%, it allows me to retain all of the 55% that is in bond or fixed investments, exposing only 45% of the portfolio to the risk of a sudden stock market drop. Conversely, if bonds dramatically drop in value, only part of my overall portfolio is exposed to the risk of a sudden drop.

I no longer fear dramatic drops in the stock market. In fact, I now look forward to abrupt drops and some of the panic that goes with it. When these conditions occur, that means that stocks have suddenly been put on a clearance sale. Bargains abound! I then begin cost averaging (buying some each month or every few months). Several years later, when economic conditions change, I am financially rewarded.

The 55/45% mix is not a magic formula. Please do not focus on that detail. Younger investors, for example, should consider a more aggressive mix that utilizes a heavier weight of equity index funds. As you get older, you might move to a less aggressive mix of assets/investments. The point is to pick a mix you are comfortable with based upon your tolerance for risk. Maintain that balance until you decide to change it based upon your stage in life or a changing personal situation.

Consider again the Great Recession, sparked by the subprime mortgage crisis, which began in 2007. Unlike the previous tech bubble crash, I was well prepared this time. I had done my homework and developed a solid plan before this unsettling period began. My savings were arranged in a diversified portfolio of financial investments in a mix that we liked.

Near the bottom of the last recession, my wife and I began a monthly buying plan that cost-averaged stock purchases (in index funds) over time. We moved our fixed investments into the equity market slowly—back to the 55%/45% mix with which we felt comfortable.

This is called rebalancing your portfolio. When stocks recovered somewhat in value, we significantly boosted our financial net worth. We also look forward to the next downturn so we can again buy stocks (via index funds) that have been heavily discounted.

We are certainly not the first people to deploy a strategy of buying stocks when they are on sale. Many people have made a fortune throughout history buying stocks when their values were depressed. For example, J. Paul Getty (born in 1892) made significant money in stocks with this strategy in his later years.

Getty made his first fortune in the oil business, beginning in the early 1920s. He started working in the business when he was young and worked most of the jobs in oil well production from the ground up. Using his father's money for financial backing, he soon made several fortunes in businesses related to oil exploration and oil wells. What is less known, however, is that he also made a fortune during market downturns later in life. When the market fell into the basement, he bought discounted stocks. When conditions improved, he was rewarded handsomely.

Each day of the recent stock market expansion, the media has given airtime to people who predict that the next significant drop in our equity markets is looming. I have watched these predictions for several decades now. They get airtime because their predictions are shocking to the public and neophyte investors.

Day after day, and week after week, the same dire predictions are put front and center by our media. Eventually, of course, they will be proven right. When our markets do fall, the mainstream media will hysterically put the dramatic drop front and center. They will report with great alarm all the damage done by the financial downturn, which typically makes matters worse.

Luckily, I no longer worry about pending market crashes. I know that business cycles (expansions and contractions of our economy and financial markets) are the norm and not the exception. Instead of lighting my hair on fire and running around in circles, I simply rely on history and economic science.

Since the 1940s, there have been 11 to 14 business cycles. That's right, 11 to 14 depending on who is counting them! As long as you have a balanced portfolio, with the mix of investments you are comfortable with, the downturn represents an opportunity for your future and not the permanent disaster that is reported by the press. (Disclaimer: this is historical information and in no way guarantees any investment returns or future market direction.) Nevertheless, I remain confident that equity financial markets will return and rise eventually. It is simply a matter of when.

Index funds are an outgrowth (in part) of the work of Nobel Prize winning economist Eugene Fama. He determined that information impacting the economy, or a particular company, immediately impacts a company's stock price and overall market prices. In other words, the financial markets operate extremely efficiently.

Let me explain briefly how this relates to you and your future. As soon as information is known about a company, it is reflected in the price of a stock or in the financial equity market as a whole. In other words, there is virtually no way the average person can get an advantage over other investors.

This is particularly true in the world of high-speed computers, automated investment programs, and high-speed internet connections that allow consortiums to make trades in an instant, when the right conditions present themselves. Fama also confirmed that no one can predict the short-term direction of the financial markets.

Translation: money managers cannot determine market direction in the short term—no matter what they tell you. Hence, there is no reason to pay higher fees for mutual fund management. Instead, efficient index funds (that mirror a particular financial market's index) with extremely low management fees give you the greatest return over the long haul.

Even a 0.5% management fee difference will cost you tens of thousands of dollars over 30 years. So why pay these fees? It is also a proven fact that higher fees (over time) do not deliver higher returns—when the fees are subtracted from your earnings. Active mutual fund managers cannot deliver the returns (long term) that you will obtain by utilizing index funds that simply pace the index.

Of course, some financial professionals (those who sell investments) will line up to disagree. They point to bubbles and other things that prove investors are irrational. An actively managed fund is the way to go this group claims—with loads of commissions (which are fees) of course.

The problem is that they fail to account for the extra fees that also go with actively managed funds. When you factor in the fees for these types of funds (buying stocks, selling stocks, commissions, loads, etc.), active fund managers do not outperform index funds over the long haul. Not because I say so, but simply because it is true.

Much to the dismay of financial professionals, more and more people are abandoning active fund managers and the investment advisors who recommend them. Actively managed funds are quickly becoming yesterday's news!

Index funds create additional safety for the investor. You don't own a few select stocks. Instead, you own the entire index of stocks. Some index funds take this philosophy even further and simply own the entire market.

The Wilshire 5000, for example, is an index that covers almost all publicly traded stocks—currently numbering over 6,000 companies. This broad market index provides investor safety from the price of a single company's stock plummeting downward (due to poor management outcomes, changing technologies, or changes in product positioning) and will not overly impact your investments. Larger market indexes also provide investor safety and insulation from corrupt managers cooking the books or outright lying about their company's financial returns.

There are plenty of sincere, totally honest, well-meaning professional money managers that will manage all your savings for about 1% annually. The selling point is, of course, the customer does not have to bother with managing these funds. One percent doesn't seem like a lot of money when considered annually.

Yet there are several problems with this 1% fee. The first problem is that you must overcome the 1% annual drain before you are able to make any money at all. Further, you are still charged management fees for your mutual funds, any stock trades your money manager makes on your behalf, and a host of other routine fees. Typically, professional investors don't do any better than an investor with a self-management strategy utilizing a balanced portfolio that features indexed mutual/ bond funds.

Occasionally, investments have a down year, making no money at all. Your investments might even lose money! Losing money for a year, or even two, is something that just happens now and then. There's no need to get too upset by it if you take a long-term view.

If, however, someone is managing your investment portfolio for 1%, you must still pay that manager. He takes his money right off the top of your pile! Better luck next year dude! No thanks! I am better off using the time-tested and proven principles I have been explaining to you and managing my own portfolio for much less.

What if I pointed out that if you educate yourself, you could easily earn about $30,000 to $50,000, or possibly more, for your effort? Just think, you can get a huge chunk of money just to read some books and do some research online in your spare time regarding money management.

Would such an offer make your self-study program more tolerable? Most people, I hope, would make the effort to secure that kind of cash. After all, if Abraham Lincoln could get his entire education through a course of self-study, then you and I can certainly do some research on a few financial issues in our spare time.

Fees are not just a theoretical discussion. You can be hit with so many fees that it can choke off or stunt your nest egg's growth. Additionally, the money spent on fees is not available to grow and compound over the years in your accounts—where it belongs.

Once you increase your knowledge and learn how to avoid unnecessary fees, you enjoy a knowledge base that makes it harder for people to scam you or take advantage of your ignorance. If you educate yourself, you certainly won't be at lunch telling your friends about what your "guy" told you about the financial markets' pending direction.

Inevitably, someone asks at this point, "Do you own gold? Our economy is on the verge of a crash, so you should own gold. We could have some kind of disaster and our economy could collapse. Only gold holds value when the dollar is devalued." The vision propagated by those who hock the gold products in the media is that America's economic crash is all but inevitable. When it occurs, you can still have money to buy the things you need by using gold. Others will be penniless, but you will have gold! This is just rubbish.

I answer the question by explaining that a number of years ago, I joined a National Disaster Medical Assistance Team (NDMS) as an intermittent federal employee. This system provides medical assistance to those areas suffering from natural or manmade disasters. My wife and I have responded to several disasters—her many more than I. We learned a number of things from our work that are priceless to us. I pass a few of these things on to you.

The first thing I learned during my service to NDMS is that if you respond to a disaster to provide medical assistance to its victims, you find yourself living inside that disaster—hence the need for large amounts of essential supplies. After this important lesson, I learned that there is a definitive dynamic to any disaster. After a disaster, there is a need for a number of things in the short term:

Needs during a Disaster:

- Safety: this includes safety from the disaster, and then safety from a few bad people who would victimize you. Typically, this is provided by getting out of harm's way and making sure your security needs are met.

- Food: food that needs to be refrigerated becomes useless in about 24 hours or less after the power is cut off. A lack of refrigeration, in turn, cuts your food supply by 3/4. This means that food is in short supply almost immediately after the power goes out.

- Shelter: protection from the elements becomes very important in disaster conditions. You must find shelter from the elements.

- Medical supplies: these supplies are an absolute requirement, as an injury in austere conditions is all but inevitable. Without medical supplies, a simple cut may get infected. An infection in austere conditions, if you are unable to get medical attention, could easily cause death or an incapacitating illness.

- Clothing: the right clothing, including dry clothing, may be in short supply.

Notice that gold is nowhere on this list. It won't keep you out of harm's way, it won't keep you warm, and you can't eat it. In fact, your gold will be useless during a disaster. No one will want gold, because they are too busy finding the above items. Obtaining gold will get you no closer to what you need during a disaster.

If a disaster is significantly prolonged, no one will really care about your gold—not for a very long time. In fact, should it later have value, the bad guys would simply take it from you anyway—hence your need for safety. I am not saying that we all turn into vicious animals after a disaster. Instead, I am saying that the bad people that already exist are unchained in an austere environment. During a disaster, it becomes easier for bad people to do the bad things they already love to do—most frequently to good, honest, decent people. Good people, however, remain good despite conditions that occur during a disaster.

Someone inevitably says, "Larry, gold is not for that. Gold is for when the dollar is devalued by government ineptitude while trying to control our economy." The same situation and conditions will still apply. If money no longer has value in our society, what can you trade to get the things you need?

Would someone with extra goods be willing to trade it for your gold—not very likely! They would want other goods that are in short supply to fill their own basic needs. Beyond manufacturing applications, gold has no intrinsic value (exactly like our dollar). Gold only has value because other people believe it does. It is a financial instrument and not the very basis of societal commerce, as some would claim.

The price and popularity of gold will go down—just as it will go up later. Does this sound familiar? It should! Like the stock market, our dollar, or any other financial investment, gold prices vary from day to day. Gold did very well during the 1970s, for example, which was a period of rampant inflation. Gold did well for a little while during the last market downturn. Currently, subject to sudden change, gold is going down while the stock market is going up and up.

Gold is rarely a good investment in large quantities and typically brings minimal returns on your cash over the long haul. The point is that gold does well during brief periods of economic unrest. To profit from a gold investment would require you to sell all your gold during an economic downturn. Otherwise, during the recovery, the price of gold simply goes back down. Obviously, selling your gold flies in the face of the economic doomsayers who insist gold is your ticket to the future when everything else crashes. Gold might perform well as a small percentage in a balanced portfolio, but that is about it.

Cash, itself, is a financial instrument and an investment vehicle as well. Cash, like every other financial instrument in the world, goes up and down in value depending upon the conditions and the events of the day. You can observe cash valuations fluctuating in several ways.

The first observation is the value of cash related to other currencies in the world. The value of cash, as compared to the Euro, for example, varies each day. Another way that cash varies is through its buying power—typically called inflation. Consider that in 1909, a new car cost $850. In 1970, a new car would run you about $6,000. In the early 1980's, a new car would set you back about $15,000. Now, a new car will likely cost you well over $30,000. These are enormous jumps. Your money buys you less and less, year after year.

Accordingly, you can conclude that the value of your cash will go down over time. This is why simply saving will never give you enough money to reach your goals. Those who only save their cash in their local bank's savings account never do as well as investors who put their money to work earning additional money.

Stocks (or company ownership) typically trend upward with inflation and become more and more expensive over time—like new cars. That means equities help you battle the drain of inflation upon your cash. Just remember that stocks, like all other investments, are subject to sudden drops in value for varying lengths of time.

How much will you need to accumulate to achieve your stated goal of leaving your wage-based job? Financial advisors offer various calculations to determine the perfect nest egg number. The number and calculations are typically designed to shock you and to get you to go along with their suggested investment strategies—which almost never involve index funds in a balanced portfolio of investments.

I can solve this equation for you, so you need not listen to their sales pitches. The amount of money you need when you retire or leave your wage-based job is as much as you can get your hands on. The caveat is that you can't and won't ever have enough money—not ever! That is an absolute fact in life.

No matter how rich you are, you will always desire more than you have. This is the natural state of being human. The trick is to determine what your income will be (or is) and reduce your expenses appropriately to live your best life within the income limitations we all face. This is not a recommendation that you go out and exhibit greedy, unethical, or illegal behavior. Everyone's responsibility is to control his or her greed. Controlling greed benefits both the individual and our society as a whole (see Chapter 9).

Consider the doctor I had lunch with at the beginning of this chapter. He had many cars, a large house, kids in private schools, and a wife that did not earn an income (a stay at home mother is only relevant to this discussion when it is considered in conjunction with the accumulation of large debt by the family). He paid a financial professional that warned him of the financial market's impending doom.

Contrast this seemingly well-to-do family with a similar family who lives in my neighborhood. In this family, both the husband and wife are doctors. Even though they both produce significant income, they live in a working, middle-class neighborhood and in a very moderately priced home. They drive an economy car and a moderately priced minivan to haul around their children.

Which of the families I have described above will work until they drop? Which of these two families will have grandparents that will retire early to help with the grandkids between trips abroad? I am sure you can figure out who will be who in the future. Even more importantly, which family will have children that understand how money impacts their lives and understand how to control its power? Which family do you want to be?

My wife's axiom of "plan ahead to get ahead" is a very relevant way to end this chapter. Your lack of financial knowledge is relatively easy to fix. Simply set a goal to educate yourself and work through the steps necessary to achieve your goal. Completing this goal can be highly profitable and is an absolute requirement to create your own amazing future.

Recommendations to get you started on your own financial education:

- Laura Adams (Money Girl) at
  http://www.quickanddirtytips.com/

- Also at http://lauradadams.com

- Also download her excellent weekly podcasts

- Eric Tyson's writing on personal finance for the Dummies series of books

- Richard Ferri and his book, *All About Asset Allocation*

- *Asset Allocation for Dummies* by Jerry Miccolis and Dorianne Perrucci

- Get Rich Slowly blog at http://www.getrichslowly.org

- Dave Ramsey and his book, *The Total Money Makeover*

- Robert Kiyosaki and his book *Rich Dad, Poor Dad*

- David Bach and his book, *The Automatic Millionaire*

- Benjamin Graham and his book, *The Intelligent Investor*

- Burton Malkiel and his book, *A Random Walk Down Wall Street*

- *The Bogleheads Guide to Investing* by Taylor Larimore, Mel Landauer, and Michael LeBoeuf

- Andrew Hallam and his book, *The Millionaire Teacher*

- William Bernstein and his book, *The Four Pillars of Investing*

TO: Present You
FROM: Future You
SUBJECT: Message from Your Future #7

Hello:

This message is urgent! It is imperative that you pay very close attention to what I am about to tell you regarding your future. Several serious economic downturns will occur during the next twenty-five to thirty years! Some of your friends who are not prepared for recessions will experience financial disaster! You, however, cannot only survive, but vastly improve your financial standing if you only listen to my directions.

Your first move is to obtain a financial education through self-study. The good news is that obtaining a financial education is easy, as many great books have been written about personal finance and investing for the neophyte. These books can be read or listened to in your car in various audio formats. A little bit of time invested in this area can yield huge financial results in your future.

There are certain financial principles that are essential:

- A balanced investment portfolio approach (based upon your risk tolerance),

- The utilization of index fund investing as your primary investment vehicles,

- Keeping all investment fees as low as possible, and

- Minimizing taxes (not an issue if you use a pre-taxed retirement account deducted from your paycheck or an after-tax Roth IRA).

The next thing we should strive to understand is that business cycles are normal. During business cycles, our economy either shrinks or expands. Each time the economy shrinks this represents an opportunity (if you maintain proper asset allocation). It is not the disaster that is typically represented by the financial media. Bring your investments back to the original asset allocations you previously chose—by buying or selling the different asset classes to bring them back to the appropriate mix. The same is true when one particular asset class takes off and becomes very valuable. Sell off some of those funds that are doing well to bring your assets back in line with your ideal mix. This strategy (called rebalancing) forces you to sell high and buy low.

PORTFOLIO

EIGHT

Risking It All

*There has never yet been a man in our history who
led a life of ease whose name is worth remembering.*

— Theodore Roosevelt

I was on a dispatch call, backing up an officer on a distur-
bance only a few blocks away. I was not driving recklessly, but
I was moving along as quickly as I safely could travel in traffic.
As I approached a busy intersection, I began to slow down for
a traffic light.

Since I was moving very quickly, my slowing was a dynamic process and not the gradual slowing normally done for
a red traffic signal. As I hit the brakes, nothing happened. The
pedal went to the floor. Adrenaline shot through my chest. I
pumped the brakes. Nope! That was not working either. Then,
my time to avoid an accident was gone and I entered the intersection at a good clip.

I was struck broadside by a car that was legally entering
the intersection. The results were pretty spectacular. I was
injured, and the people in the car that struck me were also
injured. My police car was significantly damaged and had
to be towed. Everyone's injuries, thankfully, were reasonably minor given the severity of this accident. I sustained a

back injury that still bothers me to this day. All in all, I count myself very lucky that I wasn't permanently disabled or even killed.

Every year, thousands of workers are injured on their jobs. According to the organization Disability Can Happen (http://www.disabilitycanhappen.org), a 20-year-old worker has a one in four chance of becoming disabled. Serious injury is a significant risk that all workers face, no matter what their jobs might be. The Bureau of Labor Statistics notes that every year, 112 per 10,000 workers miss work due to an injury.

At the beginning of your work career, a serious physical injury could easily derail both your **Lifetime Earning Arc** and your **Lifetime Savings Arc.** Such an injury is likely to limit the amount of money you can accumulate during the early, critical years of your savings program. An injury that takes you out of the savings game does not allow you to utilize **Financial Freedom Principle #1,** *which tells us that the earlier you begin saving and investing your wages, the greater your opportunity to harness the power of money to achieve your own ends.* The good news is, the consequences of substantial financial loss, due to injury, could lessen over time if you accumulate additional financial resources, create additional streams of income, obtain varied work experiences, and develop skills that would allow you to switch careers (or jobs within your career) to avoid financial devastation.

One of the officers who worked for me (we will call him Paul) was severely injured one morning in an auto accident while driving his police vehicle. He was actually coming to meet me at police headquarters when the accident occurred.

While Paul was driving to our meeting, an uninsured motorist turned right across his lane of travel. The crash was relatively minor, yet Paul received serious injuries that were actually caused by the air bag deployment in his police vehicle (not the initial crash of the vehicles themselves).

To summarize his story, because of his permanent injuries, he was unable to perform some of the functions required to be a police officer. One of the ways some police departments keep their budget low is to get rid of officers who are placed on the disabled list—a neat trick they learned from private industry. Our department absolutely subscribed to this cost-cutting philosophy.

There is a phrase that has become popular in police departments and several other industries (like hospitals, for example) where workers are quickly discarded if they become injured. The sad phrase is, "If you're hurt, then you're dirt."

In less than one year's time, the officer was terminated from his employment at the police department because he was unable to perform all the duties of a police officer. The police department's reasoning was that he could not be a fully functional police officer, so they were justified with this course of action. Paul's story is, unfortunately, not unique.

Luckily, however, Paul had adhered to **Financial Freedom Principle #5,** *which is to create multiple streams of income for his use in his future.* He had his own, highly successful business to fall back on—a DJ business for weddings and other special events. This was a business he had started several years before his accident. He was able to use this business to generate a full-time income for himself and his family after he was forced out of the police department.

The disabled officer did not stop there. Since he has left the department, he has gone on to create additional income streams. Paul will never be broke or unemployed in his future. He has learned business skills, marketing skills, and project management skills that now allow him to live the amazing life that he and his significant other choose.

The risk of serious injury is perhaps one of the biggest dangers that young workers face. For example, 35% of police officers in Ohio are injured and fail to complete their police careers. Consistently across the years, the jobs with the highest injury rates are nurses and nursing assistants, police or sheriff personnel, fire and paramedic personnel, and truck drivers.

In police occupations, the primary injuries result from automobile-related incidents, probably since a large portion of their work time is spent traveling in police vehicles. Nurses and nursing assistants are typically injured moving heavy patients. The best case for these injuries is a couple of weeks on leave from the job—with or without pay. The worst case is a disability, with the employer quickly moving to terminate your employment. This leaves you to fend for yourself in the confusing and bureaucratic world of workers' compensation and injury law.

Besides being mindful of safety on the job (always a priority), there are two strategies to defer the financial risk of permanent disability. **The first strategy is simply to purchase disability insurance.** You can shop around to find the best coverage at the lowest price point. Cheaper policies provide compensation only after you have already been off work for several weeks. Cheaper policies also provide you with compensation for only a limited period of time. After the specified period, all benefits cease. Depending upon the regulatory environment found in your particular state, insurance packages may or may not be available for your profession—or at costs that are feasible for you to pay.

The second strategy is to defer the risk of serious injury by using **Financial Freedom Principle #5, which is to create multiple streams of income; or, develop a job skill related to your current employment that is easily transferable to another profession.** Ideally, these skills would be in a related field that is less strenuous than your current job. It should be a skill/job that you can perform even if you are partially disabled.

A practical, personal example of Financial Freedom Principle #5 is my own choice to obtain enough formal education to enable me to teach as an adjunct professor at a neighboring university. I also taught just enough to gain experience—to make the job-hunting process easier should that plan become necessary.

Some of the officers I knew honored this principle by developing background investigation skills for use in the private sector, developing traffic accident investigation skills suitable for employment with insurance companies, or developing security related skills suitable for private security operations.

With a little thought, you can determine which of your own skills are transferable to other professions. The key is to gain a little experience in the field before such a transition might become necessary. These two strategies will substantially lower your risk of financial devastation should a disabling injury occur.

Risks, of course, are never equal. There are risks associated with daily living that are largely unavoidable—like traveling to and from your job in bad weather. But there are also what I call the **stupid risks** that people confront needlessly. Stupid risks sabotage personal lives and finances unnecessarily.

Stupid risks include drinking too much, driving a car without automobile insurance, purchasing and using illegal drugs, cheating on your significant other, smoking tobacco, high-risk thrill seeking, and other equally stupid adventures. Such unnecessary risks are obviously a sucker's bet—yet every day lives are literally disintegrated by people who take these stupid chances and lose it all.

If you don't believe these risks are a sucker's bet, let me ask you a question. How many things in life go exactly as expected? Chances are, not many things go exactly as you planned. There is almost always some deviation or slight change from the exact outcome you desired or anticipated. This is the way life unfolds.

We can control the events in the universe and twist them to our own ends—but only so much. At some point, the universe pushes back and does things its own way. Performing daredevil stunts or dangerous hobbies is a perfect example of this principle. Each stunt you perform must go exactly as you planned. Just by statistical measure alone, eventually a stunt will go slightly wrong.

I call the likelihood that something will eventually go wrong the **Significant Probability of Eventual Failure (SPOEF)**! It simply means the more times you perform a task or a job, the higher the probability is that it will deviate from the desired outcome. The more complicated a task is, the higher the **SPOEF.**

Crime easily falls into the stupid risk category. **SPOEF** sabotages the vast majority of criminals and criminal enterprises. Criminals eventually commit enough crimes that it virtually becomes a statistical certainty that one will not go exactly as anticipated.

You and I might see the element that gets them caught (such as an unexpected fact that is uncovered or a witness who surfaces) as dumb luck that favors the police. It is not luck! The root cause of the criminal being identified and captured is **SPOEF** at work. Every time a criminal commits a crime, it must go exactly the way he or she planned it. If not, the criminal is likely identified and arrested. Eventually, as in all things, one of their crimes goes sideways.

As an example, when I was a beat officer, there had been an upsurge in burglaries in the neighborhood I patrolled. In more than a dozen of these burglaries, the burglar had used a screwdriver to force open a basement window. The burglar then slid through the window and down into the basement to make his illegal entry into the home.

In each case, the burglary occurred during the daytime while the residents were at work. The houses were all built during the same time period, so the basement windows were essentially identical. This allowed the burglar to use his new-found technique over and over again. He also wore gloves, precluding fingerprint identification.

Despite my considerable effort, I could not locate any witnesses or develop any significant leads to bring the crime spree to an end. The only fact I knew was that the burglar lived somewhere in the neighborhood, as he was accurately predicting who would be away from home during his daytime burglaries.

One fine day, I responded to yet another burglary. I easily located the basement window the suspect used when he broke into the home. As I looked closely, I saw something lying in the basement window well—a brown leather wallet. Holding my breath, I opened the wallet. The wallet contained the suspect's driver's license with his current address—in the neighborhood where my burglary problem was occurring. He was rounded up in short order.

Stupid criminal you think? Maybe! After all, you can't be very smart to think burglary is a good idea. After about 13 or 14 burglaries, something was practically destined to go wrong. In this case, it just happened to be a wallet sliding from his back pocket as he slipped through the basement window.

The combination of stupid risks and **SPOEF** destroys goals, devastates relationships, and reduces the chances of obtaining financial prosperity for your future. The good news is that we are each in total control of the stupid risks that we choose to run.

We can choose simply not to do risky things and avoid many of the disastrous consequences of **SPOEF**. No, I'm not going to drink too much, because I don't want to be fat and I don't want to develop a future drinking problem. No! I am not going to drive without auto insurance, because I don't want to spend years in court and devastate my financial prosperity. No! I am not going to cheat on my spouse, because I don't want to burn down my entire domestic life, our finances, and then lose my significant other.

As a police officer, I once stopped by the hospital's emergency room on an assault investigation. While there, in an encounter totally unrelated to my radio call, I happened upon a patient who was a local university student. At the student's request, I stopped and talked with him and kept him company while he waited for emergency room test results.

The student (intoxicated at a party at the time of the incident) attempted to jump from the roof of one house to the roof of another located next door. Actually, he had completed this stunt several times before without incident. "It was always an easy jump," the student said.

As you might imagine, on that particular day this stunt turned out to be a very bad idea. He wasn't able to successfully make the leap this time! The student was unable to think through the consequences because of his extensive alcohol consumption! Now sober, the unintended consequence for him was that he was immobilized by being strapped to a hospital bed while awaiting his test results. He was in low spirits and I did my best to cheer him up before I continued on with my investigation.

If you find yourself running stupid risks, one of two things may be happening. The first is that you are unhappy. You can be unhappy without a full realization of the exact problem. If that's the case, I recommend structured and organized thinking about what exactly is making you unhappy. If you are able to figure out why you are unhappy, or why you seem to be taking risks that fall squarely within the stupid risk category, I refer you back to Chapter 2 of this book to help change your life's dynamics. You can always attack the things that are making you unhappy with direct, goal-oriented actions.

If you give some thought to why you are unhappy, but still can't put your finger on the underlying cause, I recommend obtaining assistance from a trained therapist. Counselors have an organized way of getting to the heart of the issues you are facing. There is no shame in this, as we all need help from time to time with the loads we carry in our lives.

This doesn't mean you will be in therapy/counseling for the rest of your life. A trained therapist's job is to move you fairly quickly from realization of the problem, to solutions, followed by resolution of the issues, and then to move you out of therapy. Trust me. This is a good deal for you and those you care about.

The second issues that could be causing you to take unnecessary risks are judgment or maturity issues. This is likely a symptom of other problems you are experiencing. Great accomplishments that are routinely followed by entirely avoidable disasters signal a problem somewhere in your life.

In those cases, I strongly suggest you seek the assistance of a trained therapist to help you better understand and deal with the judgment or maturity issues that seem to be sabotaging you. In fact, not seeing a therapist when you have these issues may be considered a stupid risk, in and of itself.

SPOEF also has relevance to your investments and financial security as well. When (not if) the market takes a sudden downturn, how will your investments be protected? The best way to protect your investments, as mentioned in the earlier chapter, is to protect them through a balanced portfolio of equities and annuities (equities, bonds, and a mix of investments). You also protect yourself by utilizing index funds that buy an entire index of investments. This is the strategy that will protect you as much as possible from a shrinking economy, an individual company's dramatic downturn, or a bad bet in the bond market.

SPOEF is very relevant to your health as well. Eventually you will get sick—hopefully not seriously sick. Health care insurance will allow you to quickly address health issues when, or even before, they occur. Unfortunately, health care is an ever-shifting landscape. Obtaining health care will continue to be one of the greatest challenges of our modern times.

The risk of settling for an entirely average, mediocre life that limits your achievement is also a significant life risk. The symptoms of a mediocre life include apathy for your job, unsatisfying personal relationships, lack of financial success, and a lack of any significant or life-altering accomplishments.

At the end of life's road, such people can say, "I lived an average life of mediocrity, and I was not entirely miserable." What a terrible fate this would be if you looked back upon your life and thought of it in those terms!

There are a large number of people who seem to be perfectly fine with living mediocre lives. Such an existence can be created when people simply give up after one or two failures. Mediocrity is also created when individuals follow the pack without trying to think differently or creatively about their life challenges.

For me, such a life is unacceptable! A life consisting of mediocrity is devoid of the color, flavor, and giddy joy created by your own hard-won accomplishments. A mediocre life will be filled with financial limitations as well.

It might be easier to live this way in the present, but you will sacrifice to make ends meet in the future. Waiting until the future to worry about finances means there will be no reward for the financial sacrifices you have made throughout your life. Instead, you get just a routine existence. Those who live mediocre lives are never the masters of their own fate.

Theodore Roosevelt was born on October 27, 1858. He was a sickly child with asthma, born to rich parents. Roosevelt, however, refused to accept the physical limitations his body handed him. He began a regime of physical workouts, boxing, and weight training. As a young adult, he became interested in politics and soon became a rising star in the New York political arena. He was the youngest representative to ever be elected in New York City.

Grief crashed down upon Roosevelt on February 14, 1884, when his wife and mother both died on the same day. He left New York and went into the Dakota Territory where he worked as a rancher and cowboy. After a few years, he returned to New York City and became a New York City Police Commissioner. He took his job very seriously and frequently walked the city to personally survey crime-ridden areas.

Roosevelt was later appointed Secretary of the Navy by President William McKinley. When the Spanish American War erupted, he resigned his appointment and put together a volunteer cavalry unit to fight in the war. He served with distinction during the conflict and was nominated for the Medal of Honor for his unit's charge up San Juan Hill in 1898.

He later served as vice president during William McKinley's presidency. He became our nation's youngest president when McKinley was assassinated in 1901. Roosevelt served the rest of McKinley's term, and was then elected to a presidential term of his own. He won the Nobel Peace Prize in 1906 for negotiating an end to the Russo-Japanese War. One of his greatest accomplishments (and perhaps his greatest legacy) was that he preserved our wilderness land for future generations. Roosevelt designated five new national parks and several national monuments, such as the Grand Canyon.

When Roosevelt left the presidency, he kept his life in high gear. He traveled the world and began writing books. He authored over 25 books during his lifetime. He later ran for president again, under his own Bull Moose political party.

While campaigning for the presidency, he was shot by an assassin. Suffering from a bullet wound to his chest, he still managed to give a rather lengthy speech before going to the hospital for treatment. Although he did not win this particular election, Roosevelt remained active and happy throughout his life. He died at the age of 60 of heart failure after having had enough adventures for six normal lives.

Roosevelt strongly believed that you can determine your own destiny in life. Mediocrity was never an option. He believed that his journey to create a future that was fulfilling and rewarding required significant physical and mental effort. One of the ways he prepared for this effort was to keep himself in good physical shape, a philosophy he called the "strenuous life." The strenuous life prepared not only his body, but also prepared his spirit to accomplish great things.

Records show that Roosevelt failed almost as much as he succeeded, yet he never gave up trying to create a better future for himself, his family, and the country he loved. He knew that accomplishing goals was not an easy road. Winners, if they fail, try again or draw upon their recent experiences to make better choices.

TO: Present You
FROM: Future You
SUBJECT: Message from Your Future #8

Hello:

The **Significant Probability of Eventual Failure (SPOEF)** implies that the more times you perform some task or function, the higher the chances this task or function will eventually go wrong in some unanticipated way. The more complicated the task, the higher the **SPOEF.** For example, each time a criminal commits a crime, the probability increases that the criminal will be caught for one of his or her crimes rises. Eventually, something will go wrong with one of the crimes that leads to the criminal's capture. This concept also brings to light some of the risks that you run in your life.

One of the most common physical and financial risks you face is a permanent, work-related injury that prevents you from continuing your employment. Serious injuries occur in all professions at varying rates—depending upon job duties. A serious injury could easily spiral you into poverty, particularly if you carry significant debt (financial risk) that must continually be serviced.

There are two strategies to defer the financial risk of debilitating injury brought on by the **SPOEF.** The first strategy is to work toward developing alternative sources of income, or alternative work skills, before an injury occurs. The second strategy is deferring your risk through disability insurance.

SPOEF is also why you should create a diversified portfolio. Eventually, the financial equity markets (or some other financial investment category) will fall appreciably in value. A diversified portfolio will lessen this event's impact upon your nest egg. A diversified portfolio will also increase your chances of profiting from this event in the future by buying investments at bargain prices to create future profits.

SPOEF clarifies why it is a good idea to continually improve your job skills. The chance of eventually losing your job (for some yet unknown reason) increases over time during your working career. Sooner or later, a company that employs you will be downsized, sold off, or will simply go out of business. In those cases, survival goes to those who are the most nimble, versatile, and prepared.

Finally, **SPOEF** will eventually come into play regarding your goals. Inevitably, you will be unable to accomplish some treasured goal that you have set your heart upon. The more goals you accomplish, the more likely you will fall short on one of them. When things go astray, winners try again and set new goals that are more realistic. Those who live a life of mediocrity simply give up.

One of the greatest risks in your life is the failure to live the future life that you really desire. Winners don't give up on creating a fulfilling future, but they frequently change their strategies to achieve what they want. Winners plan for the future and accept that some things will inevitably go wrong. Winners prepare for the worst, but expect the very best from life. Winners live amazing lives.

STRATEGY

NINE

The Battlefield of Workplace Ethics

*If ethics are poor at the top, that behavior is copied
throughout the organization.*

— Robert Noyce

I was a brand new police officer on my first patrol assignment, working with a group of more experienced officers on
a midnight shift. I was initially happy beyond belief to have
finally reached the goal I had set many years ago.

My happiness soon curdled like sour milk when I got to
know some of the officers working on my shift. A couple of
the officers had serious personality issues. They were rude and
disrespectful to most citizens—not to mention me.

They routinely bullied anyone unlucky enough to cross
their paths and seemed to enjoy it. They were grouchy, mean-
spirited men, who rarely had a kind word for anyone—
except for those in their inner circle who shared their embittered world view. To me, they appeared to be borderline crazy,
as they frequently flew into tirades (with citizens and others)
over seemingly minor issues.

None of their behaviors rose to the level of criminal conduct, but their actions certainly provided fodder for those who
already felt the police were jack-booted thugs. These officers'
behavior was contrary to established ethics of our profession

and contrary to our department's policies. This was definitely not what I had in mind when I took the job.

After thinking for a while, I decided I could no longer remain silent and continue to watch these guys' horrendous interactions with our citizens. I took my concerns to our shift supervisor. He quickly let me know, in no uncertain terms, that he was unconcerned about this sort of behavior.

Had I witnessed illegal behavior—which I had not—then I should document the incidents for investigation. If it was simply my opinion that the officers acted improperly under our policies, I would be better served to keep my mouth shut. After all, I was a brand new officer and couldn't possibly understand the big picture of policing. The citizens had not complained about anything, so why was I complaining to him? He also let me know that I probably wouldn't fit in with the police department very well if that was going to be my attitude toward my fellow officers.

I could have gone over the sergeant's head. The next stop in the hierarchy was my lieutenant. I felt, however the lieutenant would blindly support the sergeant without seriously examining any of my concerns. A careful investigation of the facts would demand considerable effort and probably would have resulted in negative press about the lieutenant's command. I was not certain he was up to the task, so I decided against this course of action.

I was unable to change the social dynamics on my shift and the officers' atrocious behavior continued. This situation was entirely unacceptable to me. I could not, in good conscience, continue working with this group of reprobates. I followed the only course of action open to me. I began the process of transferring from my assigned shift to another area of the city. I soon left for another shift, in another policing district, where the co-workers and supervisor were exceptional.

Some people will decry my decision as wrong. Some will say that I should have stayed and sacrificed myself (if necessary) to achieve the correct ends. They have a point, but their point goes only so far. I would certainly have sacrificed myself, but there was no hope of achieving a correct end—regardless of any sacrifice I would have made.

My dilemma was not unique. Every day, workers in all professions are faced with the same choices I faced many years ago. This is what I call the **Battlefield of Workplace Ethics**— where your ethics seriously conflict with management or co-workers. Ethical conflicts surrounding work behavior create conflicts in countless jobs and cities across our country.

In the last chapter, I referred to the **Significant Probability of Eventual Failure (SPOEF)**. This principle implies that the more often you perform some complicated task or function, the higher the chances are that this task or function will eventually go wrong. Typically, it goes wrong in some unanticipated way. This principle applies as equally to badly behaving police officers (and other working professionals) as it does to the criminals I arrested.

The officers' bad behavior continued, of course, after I left their shift. It continued until almost every one of these officers that I was concerned about got into serious trouble. The supervisor in my story had several misadventures that caused him serious career problems. Because of my very wise decision to escape this nightmare, I was not involved in any of it. In this particular situation, I felt I achieved a great victory!

Please don't misunderstand what I am implying. I am not implying that police officers will do bad things when unsupervised. The vast majority of officers are very concerned about right and wrong and strive to do what is right. Their dedication to morality occurs while working in a difficult environment and under less than clear-cut, right versus wrong circumstances.

The few that consistently don't do the right things, those unsuited for the police profession, are unleashed on the community when a supervisor fails to perform his or her duties. The same situation is true in every professional workplace. If the supervisor fails to perform, workers who have minimal interest in the job are free to act in ways contrary to their organization's needs.

I submit to you that the supervisory misdeeds in my opening story are far greater than those of the badly behaving officers. It is a supervisor's job to detect, monitor, prevent, and correct inappropriate conduct by his or her employees. Further, let me add that this particular shift had a reputation for bad behavior. If a work unit can develop a reputation for bad behavior, or not following regulatory requirements, management has already failed to meet its responsibilities.

Reputation is, in fact, the most basic ingredient in this story. It was a bad reputation that eventually led to these officers' misadventures. It was my desire not to be saddled with a bad reputation that prompted me to seek a transfer from the badly behaving shift.

It was the sergeant's reputation that eventually led to the investigations that resulted in his burgeoning career problems. A reputation is a tangible thing that impacts your daily work life—as well as your personal life. It is a valuable asset that you carry with you into your future.

In the **Seven Rules for Life Success, Rule 6** urges you to work hard to maintain your ethical and moral compass. Maintaining your ethics is not just a platitude, but a vital component of your future financial, organizational, and personal survival. In addition to very important moral, religious, and legal obligations to do the right thing, there are significant economic reasons to maintain your ethical standards.

Each of us is judged by our actions, by the results we obtain, and by the results we failed to obtain. We are judged by our interactions with others and by what we prioritize as we work to meet our life responsibilities. *The analysis of your actions while meeting life responsibilities is determined in a group-think collective at work. The analysis by the group represents your* **workplace reputation.** *You are also judged by the community in which you reside in a similar group-think process, which comprises your* **community reputation.** *These two reputations are symbiotic and create the lens by which all others view you.*

Your reputation will become either an asset or a deficit in your future. Demonstrating high standards, exhibiting good people skills, and cultivating a history of success will typically assure you of a great reputation.

A good reputation will bring you new opportunities. Based essentially upon your work reputation, your bosses will decide to present or deny you new opportunities. Based solely upon your reputation, competing companies may offer you employment opportunities in their firms.

If you are difficult to work with, fail to follow through on commitments, or frequently fail to perform at an acceptable standard, your reputation will limit the opportunities available to you. *Remember, your actions today significantly impact your future later* (**Seven Rules for Life Success #7**). Therefore, over the long haul, there are consequences for bad behavior.

Your reputation is the shortcut (or bias) that others use when they interact with you in a business environment. For example, if your reputation for working with others is one of being extremely difficult, people will generally approach you with much less patience. More demands will be made of you during your work interactions and people will generally be less flexible in their dealings with you. After all, they already expect to have problems with you from the beginning of the project.

Since they expect trouble from you, others strive to minimize the problems you will cause them when they work with you. If you have a reputation for having hidden agendas, other workers will likely expect you to double-cross them. They will be mistrustful of your actions, check your work frequently, and constantly be on the lookout for evidence of your ulterior motives.

Some people have a reputation for outright dishonesty. *If you develop a reputation for dishonesty, others will simply avoid interacting with you.* **Trust is the basic building block of all human interaction—both in your personal life and your professional life.** *Without it, very little positive interaction can occur. A total lack of trust either means no interactions at all or outright war.* For example, communities that have no trust in the police rebel against their authority through incidents of violent, civil unrest. Nations that do not trust each other typically view each other with hostility and frequently go to war.

The Chief Executive Officer (CEO) always holds the vast majority of the power in the workplace. They set the agenda and the culture for the entire organization. It is the top boss who decides what is good behavior and what is bad behavior in an organization. The CEO also dictates the best course of action to achieve the organization's ends. You don't have to be in the work world long to know that some bosses, unfortunately, are very unethical.

Problems arise for you if the boss urges you to do things that you believe are unethical. Some of you, no doubt, think this discussion is silly. Of course you're not going to do something illegal or unethical! However, when the situation actually arises, the ethics at issue may not seem so clear cut, particularly when organizational misbehavior is sanctioned or directed from the top office.

Bad organizational behavior frequently occurs when a company's survival is threatened. Organizations can be counted on to take actions designed to protect themselves. These defensive actions can range from unethical to downright illegal.

Unethical and/or illegal actions are frequently decided from a group-think perspective. When the group reaches a conclusion, the conclusion seems safe, which is a significant error in thinking. Unethical actions also commonly occur when an individual is stressed and feels his or her job is at stake. If the CEO or a Chief of Police feels their continued employment is at stake, good behavior is frequently ditched to achieve success or job security for the boss.

Leadership is closely intertwined with success, because leaders must generate interest and excitement in the quest to accomplish the work organization's goals. A good leader can take the organization's goals and persuade workers to internalize them and convert them to their own personal and professional goals. In other words, leadership encourages you to make it your personal goal to accomplish the goals set by the organization that employs you. A leader works by instilling self-confidence in their workers, encouraging an environment that honors inspiration, celebrating achievement, developing camaraderie within the organization's teams, and quickly recognizing the accomplishments of its members.

Unethical people can never be leaders! They may be in charge administratively, but it is impossible for them to lead. Ethically challenged bosses are unable to generate excitement in the organization's mission. After all, how can you have good feelings about the goals when you think you are following an ethically challenged boss?

Even if the boss is great in other ways, if his or her ethics are deficient, it will be impossible to create an environment where workers are willing to go to great lengths to accomplish the organizational goals. Therefore, failure to maintain high ethics is a shortcut to the land of mediocrity. If you are bothering to read this, then you want more for yourself. I certainly want more for you as well.

Consider Robert Noyce, who was born in 1927, in Burlington, Iowa. His family was well educated, but of moderate means. Noyce is described as a bright child who could sometimes be a bit wild. Nevertheless, he was always supremely confident in his own abilities and confident of success in every task he tackled.

As a young adult, Noyce was highly competent, likable, and a natural leader. People willingly followed him, because he was consistently confident, happy, and energetic in the projects he undertook. While in Grinnell College, he studied physics and math. During his studies, he became interested in the new transistors manufactured by Bell Labs.

After graduation, Noyce decided to attend MIT to obtain a doctorate in physics, which was a risk for him because of his family's limited financial resources. He managed to pay his bills by landing a research fellowship at MIT.

Noyce and Jack Kilby (Noyce's friend and co-worker) eventually became famous for co-inventing the microchip, which launched the personal computer industry. Noyce was soon in high demand and ran a number of companies from Fairchild Semiconductor to Intel. What makes Noyce even more amazing is the revolutionary way he treated his employees at these companies.

It was Noyce who pioneered the relaxed working environment that has become the norm for the high-tech world in Silicon Valley. Noyce broke with traditional hierarchal organizational culture, which was an almost unthinkable departure from the norm at that time. He decided to treat his employees as equals and with respect. He encouraged casual attire, he allowed casual work relationships between supervisors and workers, and he strove to keep overly restrictive bureaucracy out of his organization.

When Noyce ran Fairchild Semiconductor and other companies, he knew exactly what was going on with both his company and his employees. He was famous for walking through the plants and chatting with his workers. He knew many of the employees by name, knew their family members' names, and knew what was important to them.

He had long chats with the employees about virtually any subject they wished to discuss. Respectful dissent was allowed and opposing viewpoints were given consideration. He also recognized excellent performance by his employees every chance he could.

Given the way people talk, you can bet that anything that happened at one of Noyce's companies, or with his employees, he immediately knew about it. He took ethical behavior seriously. If something began to veer off course, he quickly detected it. Noyce was an amazing boss and a true leader by anyone's standards.

Compare Noyce's behavior and reputation to certain Wall Street financial companies in the news that are fixated on short-term gains. In such companies rules are broken, investors are defrauded, and morality is ignored. It is certainly not immoral to generate profits. In fact, this is the very thing that allows our economic system to function.

What is immoral is cheating, stealing, and double-dealing. The manipulation of financial markets, misleading investors about investments in order to make a commission on a sale, or downright defrauding investors is never a long-term strategy for success. The cheaters realize only short-term gains, but **SPOEF** is in play and typically assures financial destruction in the long term. Sure, a few people seem to get by with this behavior throughout their entire lives, but there are always consequences—even though we may not see them looking in from the outside. *Reputations have real consequences!*

I ran the property and evidence storage facility for the Dayton Police Department for a number of years. I was a member of the International Association of Property and Evidence, which promoted best practices in such units in police departments and similar organizations across the country.

When the organization published their quarterly newsletter, there were typically two full pages of police personnel who were arrested for various property room related thefts. When placed in charge of large quantities of drugs, guns, and money, some simply found the temptation too high to resist.

They stole items from the property room for personal gain and eventually went to jail or were fired—or sometimes both. Of course, everything in the property room is marked, tagged, catalogued, and is eventually audited. It was just a matter of time before **SPOEF** kicked in and destroyed their worlds.

The disgraced police property room personnel are similar to other white-collar criminals who cheat, lie, and steal for personal gain. These dishonest workers fail to understand the consequences that an arrest, indictment, or being a person of interest in an illicit white-collar scheme means to their long-term financial survival.

They traded a short-term gain (theft of something of value) for their long-term earning capabilities. Remember that trust is the basic ingredient in all human interactions. If there is no trust, no genuine interactions occur. People arrested in these cases face nothing less than isolation and ruin.

We need not single out police officers in this discussion. After the economic crisis, which started in 2007, many of the largest banks and investment companies (some of the best and most prestigious) were fined billions of dollars for lying to investors about the appropriateness and quality of the repackaged mortgages/annuities they sold.

Of course, we now know many of these financial products were worthless as investments and the banks and investment companies knew it when they resold them. Recently, many of the same banks were again fined billions of dollars for attempting to manipulate currency markets.

The layperson can only assume the leadership in these organizations is seriously flawed to continually allow such scandals to occur—regardless of the top administration's knowledge or involvement in any particular scandal. No one at these organizations is inspiring its employees to honor its customers by demonstrating ethical integrity.

Typically, legal entanglements for unethical scandals will mean financial ruin for the investor and leave the perpetrator with a limited ability to find new employment—forever. When a white-collar criminal enterprise is uncovered, it is widely reported in the media.

This means that everyone in the entire community will know of the conspirator's involvement in the illegal event or scheme—even if they were only a minor player. Additionally, you can absolutely depend on the media to portray the conspirator's involvement in this event in the worst possible light.

Police work—like so many jobs—is a constant morality test. Every day, police officers are challenged with serious moral questions. Day after day, hour after hour, the situations in which you become involved put your ethics to real world tests—with real-world consequences.

I developed a simple test over the years that I used to analyze any action I was considering to determine that action's morality. Here is the test: If avoiding the consequences of my actions will eventually require me to lie about what I have done, then the actions I am considering are immoral.

Seriously, it can be that easy. If some action you are contemplating would force you to later lie to your family, friends, co-workers, boss, industry regulators, or even the community, to avoid consequences for your actions, then don't do that particular action. Problem solved! It's solved unless, of course, your boss is telling you to do those actions anyway. In that case, find a new boss or job quickly!

TO: Present You
FROM: Future You
SUBJECT: Message from Your Future #9

Hello:

Rule 6 in the **Seven Rules for Life Success** urges you to **work hard to maintain your ethical and moral compass.** This is not an inconsequential matter, but a vital component of your financial, workplace, and personal survival. In the future, your reputation will either become an asset or a deficit in very short order.

A reputation can be defined as the interpretation of your actions by others. It consists of the results you obtain or the results you fail to obtain as you meet your life's responsibilities. You are also judged by your interaction with others and by what you prioritize in your daily life. The encompassing analysis of your actions is reached in a group-think collective that ultimately comprises your **workplace reputation.**

Moreover, you are judged in the community in which you reside in a similar group-think process—which comprises your **community reputation.** The two reputations are symbiotic and create the lens or bias by which all others view you.

In addition to your very important moral, religious, and legal obligations to do the right thing, there are also significant economic reasons to maintain ethical behavior. People who create a reputation for dishonesty have limited opportunities in the future. If someone develops a reputation for dishonesty, others simply avoid interacting with them.

Trust is the most basic building block of all human interaction—both in your personal life and your professional life. Without trust, no positive interactions can occur. Short-term gains or advantages obtained through unethical behavior place your reputation and the others' trust of you at serious risk. A reputation for ethical behavior, conversely, is a vital component of gaining trust and future opportunities.

Sometimes, unethical and/or illegal actions are decided from a group-think perspective. When the group reaches a conclusion, the conclusion seems safe—which is a significant error in thinking. Unethical actions also sometimes occur when an individual is stressed and feels his or her job is at stake.

Remember that **unethical people can never be leaders!** Others will not follow those whom they consider unethical, as trust issues prevent the conversion of the leaders' chosen organizational goals to the workers' own personal/professional goals—which is an essential process in leadership.

An easy rule to filter your actions, when the ethical path becomes murky, is to consider if you will be forced to lie about your actions to avoid consequences later. If you must lie to your family, friends, co-workers, or boss about what you did, then the action you are considering is unethical!

Should you fail one or several of the daily ethical tests we all face each day, you can expect the results to be spectacularly bad! Public allegations, humiliation, loss of job, loss of standing in your community, and loss of freedom are common outcomes.

Stealing, lying, and double-dealing take no particular talent or skill. Such behaviors comprise the very definition of mediocrity. The path to pursue is the road that leads to an amazing and prosperous life. This road is a little harder, but the destination is so much better.

CAREER

TEN

Planning To Be Happy

*The greater part of our happiness or misery depends
on our dispositions, and not on our circumstances.
We carry the seeds of the one or the other about with
us in our minds wherever we go.*

— Martha Washington

I stood in the roll call room as the chief of police spoke briefly about my career to the crowd that gathered for my retirement
ceremony. The chief and a couple of others made public comments about my contributions to our police organization over
the years. I spoke very briefly about the journey I had just completed and what it meant to me. I can't even remember what I
said now, as it all felt so surreal, but I can tell you I didn't share
with this group my true feelings about my career.

I can quickly summarize my police career by the things I
took with me as I walked out of the police station for the last time
with my wife holding my hand. I took my reconstructed front
teeth that had been broken-off during an arrest gone wrong, a
permanent back injury from a cruiser accident, and a slight case
of Post-Traumatic Stress Disorder (PTSD) from having friends
and acquaintances violently murdered on city streets.

To balance out these more severe experiences, I also took with me my lovely wife, who I met while at work, great satisfaction in having served my community extremely well for over three decades, a better-than-average understanding of our human condition, a belief in the goodness of the vast majority of people in our country, and a carefully accumulated stockpile of liquid assets.

I was absolutely certain when I began that journey so many years ago, that my goal of accumulating a million dollars would make me happy. As I mentioned previously, I had no idea at the time I was formulating my plan, that achieving this or any other goal I set was not the same thing as achieving real happiness. Goal achievement and happiness, I learned during this journey, are entirely separate deals! Achieving a goal simply creates the conditions that make happiness easier for you to cultivate and grow in your life. Having money will not, in and of itself, make you happy!

That being said, let me once and for all dispel the myth that having significant money will make you unhappy. Money, no matter how large the amount, will never cause you to be unhappy. This is an important point that tends to get lost. The popular, frequently repeated, cultural narrative is that people with money are miserably unhappy and gained it by dishonest means.

This myth is so pervasive in our culture that it seeps into our thinking and language without us even being consciously aware of it. Consider the terms filthy rich or stinking rich. These labels stem from the belief that those with money received it by dishonorable means. While money can certainly come from disreputable means, it is more likely to have been accumulated the way my friends and I obtained it—from a concentrated study of finances, hard work, and meticulous financial planning.

I have money and I am perfectly happy! My friends and acquaintances that, likewise, have accumulated wealth are also perfectly happy! It is failing to understand how to control your money that can create a considerable level of chaos and subsequent misery in your life.

For instance, consider lottery winners are suddenly thrust into the eye of a money hurricane. Most lottery winners had only moderate means prior to their sudden wealth. Due to a lack of experience with money, they have little knowledge of the potentially destructive power it will bring into their lives. Since they have not spent the time, energy, and effort required to learn how money works in their lives, they have little chance of controlling the chaos money will create if it is allowed to do so.

On my patrol beat there lived a man named John. I got to know John over time. He was a likable man who worked at several menial jobs. I would see him outside his rented home as I drove by, and would sometimes stop and chat with him. He was never a troublemaker—merely a likable man who was "just getting by" financially. With regard to money, he had little idea about how to obtain a livable wage—let alone the ability to control money's power in his life.

John suddenly inherited money—quite a lot of money from a frugal aunt. This was enough money to allow him to live comfortably for the rest of his life, probably with enough left over to allow his children to do the same. The inheritance also came with a moderately priced home in his own neighborhood, as his aunt lived very frugally and had accumulated a great deal of money.

After obtaining the money, the poor man was thrown into a chaotic whirlwind that he was unable to control. After a series of very public misadventures, he became addicted to cocaine—an immensely popular drug at the time. He spent every cent he could find on the addiction. His action ultimately left him homeless, broken, and much worse off than he started.

The **Tyrannical Rule of Money** states that *money is a requirement in everyone's lives and if you fail to control your money, then your money will certainly control you.* The unhappiness stemming from money is never money itself, but a lack of understanding of the mechanics required to control its power—before it controls you.

Assuming you have done the work necessary to learn how to control money's power, can money make you happy with your life in the future? The answer is, probably, as it depends on what makes you happy! What absolutely makes me happy (as I have said before) is the freedom my wife and I have earned in our mid-fifties!

My freedom grants me the ability to travel extensively and pursue the creative projects that I enjoy. For example, it allows me the freedom to write articles, write this book, consult with police supply companies, help my friends solve their crime/police-related problems, and work on a variety of fine art projects. The only person in the world I now must please is Mrs. Faulkner. Luckily, Mrs. Faulkner is reasonably easy to please—well proven by the fact that she married me.

Being well off financially is a big step toward creating a life that allows your happiness an opportunity to germinate. Being well off reduces the money stressors that plague so many couples. Being well off financially means reducing the day-to-day chaos so many people experience because of inadequate financial means. Being well off financially means having choices and options in your future. For example, it is then you, and you alone, who decides if you will work part-time, start your own business, or just travel around the country and have new experiences—all while still young enough to enjoy it.

A few people can manage to be happy no matter what. I think you can agree with me, however, that most people have a much harder time creating happiness in their lives when they are living paycheck to paycheck and without the freedom to choose what they will do tomorrow, let alone for months at a time. Most people are stuck working in a job long after they wish they could leave.

From this discussion, I think most people will agree with me that a certain amount of wealth will make life easier and more fulfilling. Conversely, having money, in and of itself, is not the total answer for obtaining happiness. After all, I freely admit you could have lots of money and never be happy. But I think we can now agree, as I believe I have made my case very strongly, it is not the money that will make you unhappy.

But if having lots of money is not the total answer, what does it take to create happiness in your life? To further clarify the issue of creating and maintaining happiness, I visited my friend Carla Urbanas, owner of Professional Counseling Services of Ohio, LLC.

Carla has had a long and distinguished career in many facets of therapeutic counseling. She now runs several businesses that help those who are having difficult times emotionally in their lives. She has extensive experience helping police officers, returning military personnel, and those suffering from PTSD.

Urbanas has successfully used a number of proven techniques with her clients to increase the degree of happiness they could experience in their lives. The first technique Urbanas recommends is to simply go out and have fun! Determine what it is, exactly, that you really enjoy doing. You will be happier if you make it a point to schedule these activities into your day or week.

Having a good time is a great way to brighten your entire outlook on life. Remember, having fun is a terrific stress reliever. Hopefully, your idea of fun is not an activity that is expensive. If it is, maybe you can find another activity that you also enjoy that is more moderately priced.

Urbanas also recommends a daily exercise routine for those who wish to increase their happiness. Physical activity releases endorphins, which increase your overall feeling of well-being. The first thing that police officers are generally told when they seek assistance from mental health counselors is to begin a daily exercise routine. Daily physical activity is a powerful stress reducer and it significantly mellows out your body's negative reactions to life's stressors. Exercise is also a huge confidence booster. Those who are physically fit feel more confident and in control of their lives.

The key to getting in shape is to start slow and build to more demanding workouts. Give your body a chance to adjust and begin to crave the endorphins that naturally flow from physical activity. If you over-do your new exercise program, you will dread it and not want to repeat the experience. Conversely, starting with a fast walk that builds toward more demanding exercises over time is a sure way to stick with a routine.

Urbanas also strongly recommends that all activities be performed in moderation! That means eating, drinking, sleeping, having fun, sex, and even exercising, should be done in balance with the rest of your life's activities. Too much of any one particular activity can lead to a variety of behavioral dysfunctions that negatively impact your life. Even too much exercise can be very harmful to your body.

Urbanas enthusiastically recommends taking every opportunity to laugh, as it elevates your mood. Laughing at ourselves is something we all must learn to do more often. Try to find humor in your relationships, your job, and your mishaps, and share your funny stories with your friends and family. Cultivate a sense of humor and surround yourself with those who also have a well-developed sense of humor. Laughing can make your life so much better.

In addition to Urbanas' proven techniques, Lisa and I have learned a few techniques of our own to help keep our lives in balance and maintain our happy dispositions. Consider the following tips in conjunction with those recommended above by Urbanas.

The secret weapon for creating happiness in your own life is helping other people. Nothing feels better than helping others who are less fortunate than you. This can be done by contributing money, or by volunteering in an organization whose cause you support.

Whether the cause is a homeless shelter or an animal shelter, helping others is a great way to increase your own happiness. There is a reason, after all, why those who are very rich spend so much time contributing large amounts of money and time to helping others. It is hard to beat the euphoric feeling we get when we help those less fortunate than ourselves.

Acting happy has been identified in numerous studies as a good way to increase your overall happiness. Pretending you are happy, even when you are not particularly happy, will elevate your mood. Simply resolve that you will now, from this moment forward, be happier. Set this as your goal. Write it down! Look at your goal daily. Develop an action plan to achieve your goal if necessary. Go out and act happy!

Martha Washington is a good example of a person who resolved, by force of her will, that she would be happy— no matter what circumstances confronted her. Washington led a life that was every bit as fascinating as her husband's life. Martha Washington was part of a large family—the eldest child of eight children. She was born in 1731 in Kent County, Virginia.

She was an attractive, smart woman. She married her first husband, Daniel Parke Custis in 1750. The evidence available to us today indicates it was a very happy marriage. Martha Custis had two children and wanted a large family like the family in which she was raised.

Her first two children, Daniel and Francis, both died of illnesses before the age of five. Her husband also died unexpectedly after only seven years of marriage. Before his death, Custis managed to father two more children with Martha—John and Martha (Patsy). After her husband's death, Martha was left on her own, with two children, and had to manage the

Custis estate's finances, land, and various business ventures stemming from a plantation.

George Washington, a colonel and veteran of the French and Indian War, heard about the attractive widow, Martha Custis. He resolved to meet her and boldly rode to the Custis plantation for that purpose. His boldness was rewarded, as the pair got along wonderfully from their very first meeting. The attraction between Martha and George grew very quickly. The pair was married not long after meeting each other.

Once again, Martha was happily married and genuinely adored her husband! George also loved Martha and was totally devoted to her two children from the earlier Custis marriage. (George could not have children of his own.) All records indicate George was thrilled to be a step-father and cared for his two step-children as if they were his own.

The Custis plantation and fortune were managed by George and Martha entirely for the benefit of the Custis heirs, as it was always their plan to give this part of the fortune to the Custis children. Patsy only lived to the age of 17, when she died from repeated seizures from an unknown illness.

During The Revolution, Martha Washington was very concerned for her husband's safety—particularly since she had been widowed once before and had lost all but one of her children. Martha was always an active participant in her husband's Revolutionary War effort. She did her part by spearheading a charity to buy supplies for the Continental Army's troops in an attempt to improve their horrendous camp conditions.

She also lived with her husband George and the troops during his winter encampments (war usually paused during the bitter cold winters). The troops, in turn, loved Martha for her grace and the kindness she always exhibited toward them. She uplifted the soldiers' spirits with her positive and caring manner.

In 1781, her adult, married son, Daniel, begged repeatedly to join his stepfather in the Continental Army. Eventually, he persuaded his parents to give him their blessing and he joined the Continental Army to fight for the cause of freedom. He enlisted during the epic battle of Yorktown. He soon contracted camp fever (common due to severe camp conditions, resulting from low supplies and minimal sanitation) and quickly passed away from this illness at the age of 26.

Looking back now, we can only imagine the grief Martha must have felt when she lost her only remaining child. That she lost her child for the cause of freedom, a sacrifice so many mothers made at that time, was probably of little consolation to her. The loss might have easily embittered her—but it did not. Martha strove, as best she could, to maintain a positive and happy attitude. She focused, instead, on helping her daughter-in-law raise her four grandchildren.

After the war, Martha and George greatly looked forward to returning to Mt. Vernon and private life. George, however, was swept into the presidency of the new nation he helped to create. This forced Martha into the position of our nation's earliest First Lady.

In her new position, she set the standards and protocol for the reception of dignitaries, greeting foreign ambassadors, and formal White House events. Many of the protocols Martha set so long ago still remain in use today. Martha was very popular in the nation's new capital and throughout the country. She was liked and respected by almost everyone—even by many of her husband's political enemies—because of her positive attitude.

Both George and Martha wanted nothing more than to spend their remaining days at Mt. Vernon. George flatly refused a third term so that he and Martha might return to their beloved home. Just two years after George left the presidency, he passed away in 1799, at Mt. Vernon. Martha was on her own again until she also passed away in 1802.

George and Martha Washington now lay side-by-side on the beautiful grounds of Mt. Vernon. The plantation/museum has a steady stream of visitors who wander its gorgeous grounds, tour the stately home, and pay their respects to George and Martha at their tombs. Martha managed, no matter what the situation might have been, to remain upbeat, positive, and relatively happy during her wonderfully amazing life.

The last technique for creating happiness—maybe the most important one—involves increasing your happiness by remaining positive. We all get down sometimes and that is just a part of life. Yet you must work to avoid the negativity that can seep slowly into all aspects of your life. This can be a very serious matter that demands your attention.

Police officers and other public servant professions have a high burnout rate. A symptom of burnout is hyper-negativity. Negativity is an insidious disease that can creep up on you without your even realizing it. *The more you engage in negative thinking, the more engaging negative thinking becomes.* Negative thinking is a dangerous quicksand that sucks you into its grip.

At first, negativity is appealing and can even seem to be funny, as you artfully put together witty insults to sling at various deserving targets. However, negativity soon grows until its weight becomes almost too heavy a burden to bear. Life becomes colorless, drab, and finally is crushed under the weight of negative thinking.

Negativity will never help you accomplish your goals. People who are accomplished or wealthy rarely got that way by engaging in negative thinking. Instead, those who are successful became accomplished people by maintaining a positive vision of the outcomes they desired. They also overcame various problems that blocked their progress through creative thinking. Solving problems is nearly impossible if you carry the heavy burden of negative thinking on your shoulders.

One of the easiest ways to be more positive is to surround yourself with other people who are positive. No one really wants to hang around with someone who is negative—except other negative people. Instead, we seek out close relationships with those who hold positive views of themselves, the world, and of us. Positive people inspire us! Positive people are the ones who help us believe that we are capable of accomplishing nearly anything we desire.

The very purpose of the **Seven Rules for Life Success** is to create a reasonably happy life with abundant financial resources at your disposal. Abundant financial resources buy you precious freedom and provide you with options. You can only achieve freedom by having a clear view of where it is you are headed and by creatively solving problems that block your progress. Solving your problems is much easier if you maintain a positive outlook on life.

TO: Present You
FROM: Future You
SUBJECT: Message from Your Future #10

Hello:

In order to choose the life outcomes you desire, you must make decisions regarding where it is you wish to go in your life. Choosing to have abundant finances in your future is a conscious choice that you must make. An abundant financial future is achieved by goal setting, action planning, and significant effort over an extended period of time.

Achieving your financial goals, or any goal, will not, in and of itself, ever make you happy. Still, abundant finances are much more likely to create the conditions in which your happiness will flourish. Financial abundance is certainly preferable to living paycheck to paycheck and experiencing the constant stress caused by inadequate funds. It is also preferable to working in a job you can barely tolerate in your 70s.

Here are some tips that have been proven to increase the amount of happiness you can experience in your daily life:

- Create financial abundance and learn to control money's power to prevent it from derailing your life or your happiness **(The Tyrannical Rule of Money).**

- Make it a point to occasionally have fun and be sure to schedule time for fun activities.

- Develop an exercise routine to get in shape, but remember to start slow and gradually increase exertion in your workouts over time.

- Act happy even if you are only pretending to be happy, as it will eventually elevate your mood.

- Avoid negative thoughts, negative comments, and negative people. Negativity will hinder you in accomplishing your goals and formulating creative solutions to your life's problems

- Do all activities in moderation and be careful not to let any one activity knock your life out of balance.

- Take every opportunity to laugh at yourself.

- Help other people. Helping other people does as much for you (possibly even more) than it does for them—this activity creates joy in your life.

The very purpose of the Seven Rules for Life Success is to create a reasonably happy life with abundant financial resources. This requires that you take responsibility for your finances, your life outcomes, and your ultimate happiness. Taking responsibility for your life and the vast majority of its outcomes is the path to creating an amazing life in your future. Those who do take responsibility for their lives are the ones who create outstanding outcomes and lead lives that are nothing less than amazing!

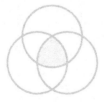

BALANCE

ELEVEN

Personal Experience is the Most Expensive Investment by Far

By three methods we may learn wisdom: First, by reflection, which is noblest; Second, by imitation, which is easiest; and third by experience, which is the bitterest.

— Confucius

Experience keeps a dear school, but fools will learn in no other.

— Benjamin Franklin

You cannot escape the responsibility of tomorrow by evading it today.

— Abraham Lincoln

The only real security that a man can have in this world is a reserve of knowledge, experience and ability.

— Henry Ford

What this power is I cannot say; all I know is that it exists and it becomes available only when a man is in that state of mind in which he knows exactly what he wants and is fully determined not to quit until he finds it.

— Alexander Graham Bell

The battles that count aren't the ones for gold medals. The struggles within yourself—the invisible, inevitable battles inside all of us—that's where it's at.

— Jesse Owens

In times of rapid change, experience could be your worst enemy.

— J. Paul Getty

I am a part of everything that I have read.

— Theodore Roosevelt

...Go off and do something wonderful.

— Robert Noyce

I was sitting in a large hotel's restaurant in Las Vegas, waiting for Lisa to join me. I had risen early, drinking a soda (my favorite form of caffeine), and going through my e-mails on my smart phone while waiting for her. This had been an absolutely wonderful trip that my wife and I had taken shortly after my retirement from the police department. We were having a great time and enjoying our newly found freedom to the fullest.

At one of the tables next to me was a woman in her mid-60s who was sitting alone. She was well-dressed and very neat. She called someone on her cell phone. Since it was noisy in the restaurant, she spoke a little more loudly than she probably would have normally. I could easily hear her side of this conversation—which was nothing less than horrific!

"Jude! Hi there! How are you? Yes… Hey, I was wondering if I could borrow $3,000. Yes… Right… I lost the money here on my Las Vegas trip this weekend. Yes, it is… gambler's bad luck, I guess. Well, you know how mad David gets about money. He just goes on and on about it. I am so tired of hearing his endless crap about money! Yes! Right! Right! I understand. Okay. Thank you so very much, Jude! I really appreciate it, because I just don't want to hear about it from David again. Thanks again, Jude! Bye, bye now!"

After this truly astonishing conversation, the woman went into the casino area attached to the hotel. Unfortunately, she was not cutting through the casino on her way to her hotel room. The woman actually returned to gambling at a bank of slot machines! She had just successfully borrowed $3,000 from a friend to cover a gambling loss and was now returning to the casino to gamble even more! I was simply stunned by what I had just overheard and then witnessed!

In addition to our human capacity to become absolutely addicted to gambling, I was astounded by her lack of understanding about how money functioned in her life. For example, she needed $3,000. There was never a time, since my early twenties, that I did not have access to a significant amount of funds for any emergency. The fact that she had to borrow $3,000 from a friend was proof that she had more issues than her gambling problem.

I wish I could say that poor woman's telephone call was the most horrible conversation regarding money that I have heard. Unfortunately, it was far from the most disturbing money conversation I ever witnessed. During my police career, I was sent on countless family-related calls. In addition to witnessing drug addictions, alcohol addictions, and infidelity issues, I also saw how money played a huge role in sabotaging couples' domestic bliss.

The most poignant example I witnessed was a woman who told me, confidentially, that she had spent all of her money—and exhausted her entire credit limit as well—on purchasing gifts for her grandkids. Evidently, none of the gifts were that important—just gifts to make her grandkids happy. Her husband had noticed this trend months prior and tried to intervene. Even her children had told her repeatedly to stop buying all this "stuff" for her grandkids. Instead of stopping, she simply hid her spending and lied to her husband about it. Now, of course, there was no way she could hide it and she knew it was about to blow up in her face. She was certain she was headed for a big fight with her husband and then maybe a divorce. After talking with her, I really couldn't disagree with her bleak assessment of her situation.

You, on the other hand, now have a chance to avoid the majority of the money mistakes made by your peers that have caused them untold misery. For example, you know that you can achieve excellence if you first decide upon your goals and then take positive action steps to obtain your personal and financial dreams. You know that you can, if you will only decide to do so, gain control of your destiny through your own continuous efforts. You have now read that the reason goal-setting is very important is because you are totally responsible for the vast majority of your life outcomes.

You now comprehend that controlling your money is an essential life skill that you must master quickly—or your money will soon have you dancing to its own bitter tune. You know that money does not care about you and will likely destroy your chances for happiness if you fail to control its significant power in your life. You have read that your greatest asset in your quest to control your money will be educating yourself on the subjects of personal finance and investing. Money, after all, will always be a constant in everyone's life.

A job is necessary, because you must fund your life. With that understanding, you now recognize that the reason for you to have a job is to make money—not to achieve an altruistic goal. If an altruistic goal were the most important aspect of a job, you would simply be volunteering your time and energy to your community and forget about earning money.

Furthermore, you learned that you can no longer expect an employer to be loyal and take care of you, so you must consistently work to develop marketable skills to increase your earning potential and create additional opportunities. Along with this fact is the grim reality that you cannot count on the government or a pension fund to financially bail you out of your financial failures in your old age.

With the information contained in these pages, you have learned that the earlier you can get money into your investment accounts, the easier it will be to achieve your financial objectives by harnessing the power of compounding interest. You have also seen clear examples that illustrate the importance of controlling your spending, because it is so easy for anyone to outspend their income.

Controlling your spending is also vitally important, because you now know that you have a limited work life and your earnings' clock is ticking as you read this. You now know that you cannot squander your limited funds on adult toys or other frivolous possessions and still accomplish your important goals.

You now realize the economic boost that comes from treating others in an ethical and honest manner. You have also seen the significant consequences that follow for those who fail to maintain a good reputation within their communities. You have read how dishonest, short-term gains will rarely outweigh the advantages (or earnings) gained through ethical behavior over life's long haul.

Finally, you know that if you can manage these strategies for creating an amazing life, you will live a life of unparalleled freedom with a significant opportunity to increase your future joy and happiness. Money will not bring you happiness, but it will bring about the conditions in which you can likely grow and cultivate happiness. In short, by implementing the concepts you have read in these pages, you can build a life that few are ever lucky enough to experience.

Intellectually, knowing all these facts and the accompanying life strategies is not the same as incorporating the concepts into your daily living. We can learn things intellectually or we can learn things from personal experience. Personal experience will be much more costly than intellectual learning that we incorporate into our habits and behaviors.

So many times we refuse to incorporate new strategies or concepts into our thinking until we suffer bad outcomes—sometimes repeated bad outcomes. This is the very reason children don't listen to their parents until they suffer a few scrapes and bruises earned from ignoring their parents' directions, "Don't run here!" Learning only through personal experience is a human tendency that creates so many unnecessary hardships.

In our family, we have a phrase that we typically add after we give advice, "Do you know how I know that?" It is a rhetorical question that means that we have made a mistake related to the issue and have learned how to avoid a bad outcome in this particular area. Of course, hardheaded people may only learn things in the very hardest of ways! The hardest way, by far, is through personal experience. In fact, learning things through experience could even be fatal!

At the beginning of this book, we discussed how you are the captain of your own ship. You are sailing your ship through the dangerous waters ahead. Off the port and starboard lay dangerous shoals that could destroy your ship. The shoals may be mere meters away from your ship's intended path. If you wish to safely navigate the waters ahead, you must consult the charts created by the captains who sailed these very same waters before you.

Did you stop to think that the charts that you were consulting have been created from both the failed attempts and successes of those who sailed these waters in the past? The disasters other captains experienced in these waters were used to create the wonderful charts that you now have the opportunity to consult.

You have only to follow the charts, built upon the sunken ships of the past, to avoid the disasters that have occurred in these waters. Sailing safely in dangerous waters will allow you to leap forward and achieve much greater success than your peers. It will be your peers who will scrape and damage their ships on the ragged and harsh shoals of personal experience.

You need never follow others' charts of course! You can simply disregard the hard-won experiences recorded on the document. You may go any way you like. In the end, we all have the gift of free will. This is certainly what you will do if you are one of those people who can only learn through his or her own personal experiences.

Similarly, you have read messages from your future. You now know these messages were written by the rough hands of personal experience. You also know these messages were verified time and time again through the historical accomplishments and experiences of others who changed our world for the better. Every generation and every person in each generation need not relearn everything from personal experience. If you were freed from the most common misadventures in life, think how much more you could accomplish. I know that in my life, if I would have had the opportunity to consult messages from my future, I could have easily accomplished twice, or even three times what I accomplished—in every aspect of my life. What an opportunity that would have been!

So Captain, the question is how will you sail your ship through the waters that lie ahead? Will you consult the charts of experience, verified by the past successes and failures of others, and successfully navigate the waters of your future? I recommend you follow your messages from your future, make your life better, make your life happier, become more successful, and create more prosperity. Live a life that will be nothing less than amazing!

TO: Present You
FROM: Future You
SUBJECT: Message from Your Future #11

Hello:

We have covered a lot of material in the important messages I have sent you from your future. You have now read the information necessary to create a very successful life—both now and later. In the present, however, you are faced with a very important choice. That choice revolves around what kind of person you are going to be. Are you a person that can only incorporate life's lessons through their own personal experience; or, are you a person that can read information, consider it, and then incorporate what you have learned into your life? It will be so much easier for you, more prosperous, and more fulfilling if you can live a life that values the hard-won experience and knowledge of others.

As humans, going through life, we develop a sense of permanency. We feel as if this is our life and this is how our life will always be. We subliminally believe that our life will remain unchanged forever. This is one of the reasons why people build houses on flood plains. When it does not flood for several years, or even several decades, we easily forget that it will flood in these locations in the future—it's just a matter of when. We build houses on flood plains because we expect time and our life to continue as it has for the last several years without disruption. This is, of course, merely an illusion. Life changes quickly, sometimes drastically, and typically with little warning.

Your future will come! You will be older. Your future can be what you created through your conscious intentions and by the sheer force of your will, or by drifting where the tides take you by chance. Your fate lies totally in your own hands. You can do what feels good now; or, you can understand that time flows quickly and waits for no one. This fact can either intimidate you, or you can embrace it. I chose to embrace it, and created an amazing future. What is your choice for your future?

MISSION

Larry Faulkner

AUTHOR

Larry Faulkner's 32-year police career began at the Dayton, Ohio Police Department in 1981. He was promoted through the ranks and eventually retired as a Major. During his career, Larry was awarded the Department's Distinguished Service Award for heroism, the Joseph T. Cline Award for customer service, and the Award of Merit twice for outstanding service to the community. Additionally, he and his team of police and community members garnered international attention for various community policing initiatives.

Larry and Lisa were married in 1992. The couple set a goal of achieving financial independence early in their relationship. Together, the couple raised their three boys to become financially independent and successful adults in their own right.

After extensive research and experience in saving and investing, the couple achieved significant success in creating financial abundance. The knowledge Larry gained has allowed him the opportunity to educate other police officers and public safety professionals on saving, investing, and goal achievement. He also developed an educational class that encouraged new police recruits to save and invest their money from the beginning of their careers, so they might also achieve financial independence.

Larry and Lisa retired from their old jobs in their mid-50s with over a million dollars in financial assets. Larry continues educating public safety personnel on personal finance. The couple now set their own schedules, come and go as they wish, and enjoy traveling extensively across the U.S. and abroad.

To learn more about achieving your own goals and creating financial independence in your life that few people are lucky enough to experience, visit **messagesfromyourfuture.com.**

CPSIA information can be obtained
at www.ICGtesting.com
Printed in the USA
FSOW04n0406280416
19772FS